TRANSFORMING DARKNESS INTO LIGHT

TRANSFORMING DARKNESS INTO LIGHT

A Holocaust Survivor's Lessons in Fighting Hate

RABBI PHILIP LAZOWSKI WITH SUZANNE BATCHELOR PINKES

BLOOMSBURY ACADEMIC
NEW YORK • LONDON • OXFORD • NEW DELHI • SYDNEY

BLOOMSBURY ACADEMIC
Bloomsbury Publishing Inc, 1359 Broadway, New York, NY 10018, USA
Bloomsbury Publishing Plc, 50 Bedford Square, London, WC1B 3DP, UK
Bloomsbury Publishing Ireland, 29 Earlsfort Terrace, Dublin 2, D02 AY28, Ireland

BLOOMSBURY, BLOOMSBURY ACADEMIC and the Diana logo are trademarks of
Bloomsbury Publishing Plc

First published in the United States of America 2025

For legal purposes the Acknowledgments on p. viii constitute an extension
of this copyright page.

Cover design: Chloe Batch

All author proceeds to go to non-profit organizations that provide Holocaust and genocide
education or otherwise combat hate.

Bloomsbury Publishing Inc does not have any control over, or responsibility for, any third-
party websites referred to or in this book. All internet addresses given in this book were
correct at the time of going to press. The author and publisher regret any inconvenience
caused if addresses have changed or sites have ceased to exist but can accept no
responsibility for any such changes.

A catalog record for this book is available from the Library of Congress.

ISBN: HB: 979-8-7651-6774-8
ePub: 979-8-7651-6775-5
ePDF: 979-8-7651-6776-2

Typeset by Deanta Global Publishing Services, Chennai, India

For product safety related questions contact productsafety@bloomsbury.com.

To find out more about our authors and books visit www.bloomsbury.com
and sign up for our newsletters.

This book is dedicated to three women whom I love, cherish, and admire and from whom I have learned so much:
To my beloved mother, Chaya Gitel, of blessed memory, whose love saved my life while sacrificing her own at the hands of the Nazis;
To Miriam Rabinowitz, of blessed memory, whose faith, courage, and kindness knew no bounds;

and

To my wife and soulmate, Ruth, who has been the love of my life for the past seventy years. Her steadfast devotion has been given with all her heart and soul, and she has been the best wife, mother, and grandmother that anyone could ever imagine. I could never have accomplished what I have without Ruth by my side, and we are both blessed to have a life filled with love and admiration for each other and the community that we serve.

CONTENTS

ACKNOWLEDGMENTS

This book became a reality only through the prodding of my son Alan (not too gently). I told him that I had written too many books, and it was enough. However, for the love of my son, I could not refuse. So, God blessed me with a lady named Suzanne Batchelor Pinkes, who offered her kindness to help me with the writing of this book. Kudos and special gratitude to Suzanne for her invaluable contributions in helping write and edit this book. This would not have come to fruition without the aid and advice of my literary agent, Rita Rosenkranz, and the support of Ashley Dodge, Laney Ackley, and the entire team at Bloomsbury Publishing. I am grateful for their confidence in me and interest in this project. Additionally, thank you to Dr. Leon Chameides, my dear friend and fellow Holocaust survivor, for his sage advice, wise counsel, and thoughtful attention to detail. I also want to express my heartfelt thanks to Jeffrey Rosenberg and Rev. Susan Izard for reading the manuscript and offering valuable suggestions. Alicia Hernandez has been my steadfast administrative assistant and has always remained cheerful, despite my sometimes indecipherable handwriting, for which I am very grateful. I am also thankful for the help of Genesis Cordero and Gail Blanc. Thank you to my family, friends, and community for their encouragement. Finally, I want to thank all the Holocaust survivors who have had the courage to tell their stories and remind the world of where hateful ideas can lead, as well as all those who have stood up in the face of hate to build a more just and peaceful world. All author proceeds of this work will be donated to organizations that promote Holocaust and genocide education and otherwise work to fight hate, antisemitism and injustice.

FOREWORD

I kissed my grandfather goodbye.

I was rushing—late for a plane—and had to hustle out the door. He was battling cancer. His once-grand frame was now shrunken and weak. There were signs of early dementia. He could no longer make it up the stairs to his bedroom, so we'd made him one downstairs.

Still, when I entered the room, he cracked a joke.

"How you doing, Granddad?"

He smiled, reached for one of the many pill bottles by his bed, and said, "Say hello to my little friend."

I laughed, leaned down, kissed him, and said, "I love you, Granddad."

As I turned to leave, he called after me, his voice fragile but clear:

"I love you. I love your children and grandchildren."

I paused, confused. I didn't have children—let alone grandchildren. Was he mistaking me for someone else? Was this a flicker of dementia? I didn't have time to clarify. I had a plane to catch.

We never know when a moment will be the last—with a loved one. The last joke. The last embrace. The last kiss.

This was mine.

The final time I saw my grandfather. The final words we shared. The final time I felt his warmth and told him I loved him.

When I got the news of his passing, I was in a car back home in Newark, New Jersey. I pulled over and wept. I felt crushed under the weight of loss. My grandfather was larger than life—a man who rose from the deeply segregated South to a wartime job on the assembly lines of Detroit, building bombers for the fight in Europe. He and my grandmother became entrepreneurs: a gas station, a laundromat, a pool hall. They moved to Los Angeles and built a life of economic success.

By the time I came along, they were helping raise their seven grandchildren—taking us across America in a pea-green mobile home they called The Green Dream.

My grandfather was one of my earliest heroes. He was my living history. He helped me fall in love with America, not for its perfection, but for its promise. He showed me that a life of love, hard work, and constant service to others wasn't just noble—it was joyous.

Sitting on the side of the road that day, my mind returned to his final words. Suddenly, they made sense—and gave me comfort.

My grandfather lived a life of such powerful, persistent love that it could stretch beyond time. He loved so fiercely, so thoroughly, that even generations yet unborn would one day feel the warmth of his care. He loved me—and he loved my children and grandchildren. Even if they hadn't yet come into the world, his love was already reaching for them.

Later, I learned something about the universe that felt like a revelation: the light we see from the sun is not the sun as it is, but as it was—eight minutes ago. That's how long it takes light to reach the Earth. The stars we see shining in the night sky? They are billions of light-years away; many of them died out long ago. But we still see them because their light—what they gave off while they were alive—goes on.

And so it is with us.

In both the laws of physics and the laws of spirit, the warmth, energy, and light we give off in life continue long after we're gone. The greater our love, the brighter our light, the longer our radiance lasts. The truest immortality isn't in how long we live—but how deeply we shine.

By that measure, Rabbi Lazowski is a supergiant—a celestial beacon in the constellation of our world. A nova. A North Star.

I first heard his story from his son, Alan.

We met for the first time in a conference room in New York. I take a lot of meetings in my job—but this one was different. Alan, a successful businessman, carried himself with no airs. His warmth and humility belied his stratospheric accomplishments. Before I knew it, we weren't talking about politics or policy. We were talking about life, faith, family, and what it means to live a life that matters.

And then he told me about his father.

The story struck me as cinematic—so poetic, so profound, that I found myself tearing up before a man I had only just met. As Alan spoke, I felt his father's presence in the room, radiating through him. They lived different lives, but it was clear: Alan was his father's son.

I'm a Black Christian man. Alan is a Jewish son of a rabbi. After that conversation, Alan became my brother.

This is an extraordinary book. And I believe that if you read it with an open heart, if you allow its spirit to speak to yours, then Rabbi Lazowski may become for you what he became for me: a guide, a light, a father figure in the broader sense—a soul whose example can ground us in virtue and challenge us to be better, love harder, shine brighter, so that generations after us may navigate by the light we leave behind.

As a Christian, I've long been drawn to the stories and traditions of Judaism. I believe deeply in the kinship of the Abrahamic faiths—Judaism, Christianity, and Islam. In the African American tradition, we have drawn richly from the Torah—especially in our long, ongoing struggle to make America a more just and loving home for all its people.

One of my favorite writers is James Baldwin. In *The Fire Next Time*, Baldwin ends a painful, prophetic, and necessary book with a call not to despair, but to dare—to believe in what may seem impossible. He writes of the urgency of now, of the duty to love with both tenderness and truth, and to change the world not through vengeance, but through vision—and always love in action.

When I think of Rabbi Lazowski's life—what he endured, what he built, how he loved—I think of Baldwin's final charge. It is as if Baldwin, too, was pointing us to a North Star. To what is possible.

Yes, we live in difficult times. But we must expect no less from ourselves than this: to show that love—courageous, unyielding, unbowed—still has the power to save us. That the fire of our compassion can light the path to a better world.

It is a tall order. But, as Baldwin said:

"Everything now, we must assume, is in our hands; we have no right to assume otherwise. If we—and now I mean the relatively conscious whites and the relatively conscious blacks, who must, like lovers, insist on, or create, the consciousness of the others—do not falter in our duty now, we may be able, handful that we are, to end the racial nightmare, and achieve our country, and change the history of the world.

"If we do not now dare everything, the fulfillment of that prophecy, recreated from the Bible in a song by a slave, is upon us. God gave Noah the rainbow sign, no more water, the fire next time."

Cory Booker, United States Senator, New Jersey

Introduction

This book focuses on my personal reflections on what it means to fight hate and bring light to darkness. Light radiates a sense of optimism and undying love for a better world, community, and human beings. In the face of the challenges of hate and antisemitism, light brings vision and a noble inspiration for self-improvement and the advancement of society. This book is also very personal. I have not hesitated to include my experiences during the Holocaust in the Second World War, and afterward. I learned that to survive, we need miracles and I can tell you that miracles happen every day; some are blended into nature, and some are visible and distinct.

When I was ninety-three years old, I was diagnosed with metastatic cancer. I was told I had two months to a year to live. Several months later, my cancer had receded, and my doctor said to me, "Rabbi, you must have friends in high places." That may be, but what I do know is that I have received an outpouring of support and prayers from both Jews and non-Jews, and these prayers have been answered. This is one of many miracles that have brought light into the dark moments of my life.

The truth is, I shouldn't have made it past my teenage years. You see, I was born in Poland in 1930 into a comfortable, traditional, and loving Jewish family and community. We lived in a village, Jews and non-Jews alike, going to school and working alongside each other in relative harmony. We were happy.

* * *

The town that I grew up in, Belitza, was, at the time, near the border with Russia and not far from where we lived was a Russian military air base. This base was used to train Russian pilots. These airmen would periodically come into our town, and they were recognizable because of their customary shaved heads. Our little town was located at an important geographical location, near a junction with the Nieman River, which was used to send lumber from the local forests to the Baltic Sea. Our location, near the Russian base and the river, made our town of special interest to both the Russians and the Nazis. Looking back, I realize it was only a matter of time before the two would engage with each other in our midst. This happened when the Nazis arrived in 1941, and the Russians killed three of them.

One evening shortly afterward, the Nazis stormed into town, demanding that everyone come out of their houses. We were terrified but obeyed their commands. We were huddled together outside: my mother, Chaya Gitel, holding the youngest, my sister Rachel; my father, Josef, who was bald, was holding the other baby, Aaron; and I stood holding the hands of my brothers, Abraham and Rachmil. We had no belongings save the clothes on our backs. Our neighbors were in the same situation and were also outside with us, fearful of what would happen next. Then the Nazis began to set fire to the houses, and our home was the first to be set aflame.

Because my father was bald, the Nazis accused him of being a Russian from the military base. They threatened to shoot him right then and there. We children were so scared and felt so powerless. But my courageous mother shouted that this was her husband, he was not a Russian, and begged that he not be killed. For some reason, this seemed to be enough, and the Nazis spared him. But to our horror, they immediately shot another man standing next to my father. This was the first time I saw someone murdered. It would not be the last. It would also not be the last time that my mother saved someone's life.

I was eleven years old.

* * *

The Nazis and their collaborators confiscated all our town's Jewish businesses, including my family's, burned our homes, and expelled us to a ghetto, a waiting room for death. This was the fate of all the Jews in our village and the larger surrounding area. The mass killing of Jews in the Second World War, known as the Holocaust or, in Hebrew, the *Shoah*, spawned the concept of "genocide." The word "genocide" was coined in 1942 by Polish Jewish lawyer Raphael Lemkin and was defined as "a coordinated plan of different actions aiming at the destruction of essential foundations of the life of national groups, with the aim of annihilating the groups themselves."[1] The United States Holocaust Memorial Museum further defines genocide as "acts committed with the intent to destroy, in whole or in part, a national, ethnic, racial or religious group."[2] The coordinated and systematic destruction of Jewish communities and mass murder of Jews by the Nazi regime, a genocide, resulted in the deaths of more than two-thirds of the Jews of Europe and a third of all the Jews in the world. In all, six million Jews were murdered.. Each of these was someone's mother, father, grandparent, child, sibling, friend, or loved one who was murdered by being shot, gassed, worked to death, burned, starved, abused, and experimented on. Among the victims were over one million children who, before the Nazi regime, attended school, went to synagogue, played with toys, socialized with friends, and had dreams of what they would be when they grew up. The light of all this potential was snuffed out. This was the darkest time of my life.

As you will read later, humanity has a very long (nearly three thousand-year) history of violent hatred targeting the Jewish People, or what is called antisemitism. The Holocaust was the apotheosis of this antisemitism. As a child, I witnessed fellow Jews being beaten, tortured and shot, buried alive, a baby on its mother's breast being speared by a Nazi bayonet—unthinkable horrors that I can never forget. The Nazis were like animals, or worse, since they seemed to kill for pleasure. Rabbi Yaakov Emden (aka Ya'avetz), one of the most famous rabbinic thinkers of the eighteenth century, wrote that the survival of the Jewish People over three millennia was the greatest miracle that God ever performed, eclipsing all others. He could not have imagined the Holocaust. But again, we survived.

I feel compelled to write this book because of a recurrent and increasing torrent of hateful attitudes, words, incidents, and violence directed at Jews and the Jewish community—something that I never thought I would see in my lifetime. In the United States and elsewhere, increasing antisemitism was already on track in 2023 to be the highest on record *before* the deadly attack by the terrorist organization Hamas on innocent civilians in southern Israel on October 7.

Years earlier, on October 27, 2018, a man with a gun and a deep belief in antisemitic conspiracy theories killed eleven worshipers and wounded six others at the Tree of Life Synagogue in Pittsburgh. This was the deadliest attack on Jews in American history. The attack by Hamas five years later was the deadliest attack on Jews anywhere since the Holocaust. That morning, twelve hundred people were brutally murdered while attending a music festival or simply going about their daily routines at their homes. The killed included forty-six Americans and innocent civilians from thirty other countries, the elderly, women, and children. Many women were raped, bodies of the dead were dragged through the streets and defiled during this spasm of violence. In addition, 254 people, including 12 Americans, were taken hostage in Gaza. They included men, women, children, and the elderly. Scores of people remained in captivity for well over a year, and many hostages were murdered or died in captivity. Hamas terrorists emerged from the darkness of their underground tunnels and returned their captives to the same dark spaces. When I heard about what had happened, I was reminded of what I had personally experienced more than eighty years ago. This was a new pogrom, and the murderers danced with glee and, shockingly, so many others in the world were dancing with them. Was this going to be a new Holocaust?

I believe that this event, had it happened to any other group of people, would have engendered an outpouring of support and condolences. However, within days of the attack and before the government of Israel militarily responded, protests exploded around the world.[3] In many cases, these protests praised and glorified the actions of a terrorist organization and placed blame on Israel for the deaths of its people. While some protestors were concerned about the policies and decisions of the Israeli government, such criticism alone is not antisemitism. In democratic countries, we all criticize our governments. However, many of the protestors demonstrated with hateful signs, images, and slogans that targeted the Jewish People as Jews, no matter where in the world they lived. This is antisemitism, and I was disturbed at the level of vitriol openly expressed, tolerated, and even supported, including the open support for terrorist organizations. And I was shocked at the level of ignorance about Israel and the Jewish People displayed by so many of the protestors. This is a dark time.

So, at ninety-five, I believe that my life's experiences have taught me about antisemitism and hate, and, even more importantly, I have learned a lot about building peace.

In the Jewish religious tradition, we recite a prayer, the *Amidah*, multiple times every day, and in this prayer, we give thanks for the "miracles that daily attend us." I survived the Holocaust because of miracles. As you will read in this book, my life was saved by the courage of my mother and again by that of a stranger, and the actions of sacrifice and courage by yet another young mother spared me while I was hiding in the woods during the war. A request for care from a young victim of sexual assault saved my life after I was comfortably living in the United States, and the courage and support of so many in my life have allowed me to live and thrive, sometimes in ways that feel miraculous.

After surviving the Holocaust, I was fortunate enough to come to the United States and become a rabbi. So much of how I approach my life and profession is informed by having lived through one of the darkest periods of human history. I, and many others, experienced tremendous loss and suffering because of hatred that, in a few short years, moved from words, attitudes, and ideas into deprivation of rights and then into mass murder. This violence was not limited to the Jews of Europe. The Nazis also systematically murdered people with opposing political beliefs, members of the LGBTQ community, people with disabilities, the Roma People, and more. My life's work has been to counter antisemitism wherever it is expressed and to fight against all forms of hate. I learned far too early that hatred and violence toward the Jewish People are bound up with hatred of so many others, and that fighting antisemitism benefits people far beyond the Jewish community.

Pursuing and working toward peace has been part of my everyday work. In the *Amidah*, we pray for peace at least five times. The *Kaddish Shalem*, as well as the Mourner's *Kaddish*, prayers that are recited multiple times every day, conclude with a request that God grant us all peace. The blessing that we bestow on our children every Sabbath, or *Shabbat*, asks that God give them peace. In the *Pirkei Avot* (Sayings of the Fathers), our sages remind us that the world stands on three things: "on justice, on truth and on peace," and the great Rabbi Hillel urges us to love and pursue peace.[4] We also regularly pray for the United States, asking that "citizens of all races and creeds forge a common bond in true harmony, to banish hatred and bigotry." [5] As the *Midrash* says, "Great is peace for it is equal to all the work of creation. . . . Great is peace for the name of the Holy One is peace."[6] Fighting antisemitism and hate and striving for peace are central to my life and to what it means to be a part of the Jewish People. In this effort to pursue peace, we fulfill the task of being a light unto the nations.[7]

After surviving the Holocaust, becoming a rabbi, and living a long life, I did not anticipate that I would feel compelled to write about the need to fight a resurgent antisemitism in the United States and around the world. My hope was to talk about antisemitism as something relegated to the dustbin of history. Of course, my dream has always been that another Holocaust would never happen, that the motto "never again" had meaning for everyone, and that humanity would have learned, by now, not to hate but to live in peaceful coexistence. But the rapid rise in antisemitism over the past ten years, the attack by Hamas, and the ensuing explosion of antisemitic words, phrases, attitudes, harassment, vandalism, and violence inspire me to write of my life's experiences in fighting hate.

I want to acknowledge that this rise in hatred has made many Jews feel afraid. Because our history is filled with three thousand years of acts of brutal and violent hate, it is natural that when something like the Tree of Life shooting or the October 7 massacre happens, we react with fear. This fear can be an important motivator. During the Holocaust, I could not have survived if I did not have a fear mechanism to sound the alert when our lives were daily threatened. I had to learn the sound of the wind, the grass, the trees, the animals, and the hostile enemy, and be able to distinguish between them. The Nazis hunted us relentlessly.

What was my salvation? I begged God for help. Throughout history, Jews have turned to the Bible to seek fortification against the terrors of life. The psalmist said, "Heal me, O Lord, for I am frightened." And Isaiah reminds us that God said, "Fear not, for I am with you."[8] And in the Torah, it is written, "Be strong and courageous. Do not be afraid or terrified because of them, for the Lord your God goes with you; he will never leave you nor forsake you."[9] All of these verses helped me when I was living in the darkest of times, and we can all call on them for inspiration. We must never give up hope. As we read in Psalm 23, "Though I walk through the valley of the shadow of death, I shall fear no evil for Thou art with me." This is how we meet the challenges of life that make us feel afraid. We can master fear through faith—faith in the worthiness of life and the trustworthiness of God; faith in the meaning of our pain and our striving, and confidence that God will not cast us aside but will use each of us as a piece of a priceless mosaic in the design of His universe.

This fear can also motivate us to remember the importance of speaking up when hate is in words and attitudes and before it is expressed in deadly action. We can take this moment as an opportunity to stand up together in unity. A source of hope is the fact that fear is temporary, and when we can keep our fear at bay, we can have hope and optimism. This allows us to act. However, Divine assurance for our survival encompasses our involvement. Our forefathers and foremothers did not sit back with folded hands in apathy. That is what the sages meant when they interpreted the verse, "And all your children shall be taught about the Lord, and great shall be their peace,"[10] by saying, "Call them not 'your children' but 'your builders.'"[11] We must become builders of the world we want because when it comes to building the peaceful world we seek, "It is not your duty to finish the work, but neither are you at liberty to neglect it."[12]

Therefore, despite the darkness around us that allows antisemitism to grow, be not afraid; have faith and hope. Know that a single candle lights up the darkness, and when we are connected with each other, we are a powerful light. Together, we are stronger and better able to combat the corrosive impact of antisemitism and all hate. From the tiniest spark, we can join with others to create the brightest beam. I lost my mother and three siblings to the Nazis' vile hate, and I learned how to survive for two years hiding in the woods. I experienced miracles, faced fear, drew on my faith, and had hope. I never gave up. We live in a world where there is plenty of darkness, and I am living proof that we can use our strength, courage, and resilience to emerge on the far side of darkness into the light of a new and better day.

In this book, I will share the stories, Jewish texts, and lessons I've learned from my lifelong effort to combat hate and build peace. I will start with a brief description of antisemitism and how it is expressed. While I have much "lived experience" of being the target of hate for being a Jew, I am not a scholar of antisemitism, so I will also provide suggestions for further reading. The remainder of the book will be a discussion of eight thematic areas connected to stories from my life and scripture that help us to fight antisemitism. First, we must know and understand that the history of hatred targeting the Jewish People is not limited to the Holocaust. It is also important to know who the Jewish People are—that we are more than a religion and that we are diverse in every way. As a rabbi, the topic of faith is very important to me, and I believe that it is critical in fighting hatred because it helps keep hope alive. In my experience, I have found that friendship is a powerful force in combating antisemitism that all of us can use. In addition, I have spent a lifetime educating young people about hate through my story of surviving the Holocaust. Each of us can also summon the courage to stand up to hate and bigotry, helping ourselves and others to build a more peaceful world. Understanding what Zionism is and the ancient connection that the Jewish People have to the land of Israel is also important in dispelling some of the ignorant antisemitism I have seen recently. And finally, building a strong Jewish community and making deep connections with other groups as allies is fundamental to fighting bias and bigotry of all kinds.

I will leave you with suggestions on how to incorporate these ideas into your life, including taking any number of specific actions. Even if you commit to doing just one thing, that is one more than you did before. That one action could be enough to change the world. As the sage Rabbi Hillel said, "If I am not for myself, who is for me? But if I am only for myself, what am I? And if not now, when?"[13]

1

What Is Antisemitism?

During the Holocaust, I suffered terribly myself and saw others suffer. As a twelve-year-old alone in the world, I saw unimaginable atrocities. I wondered, why do people dislike me just because I am a Jew? At the age of six, I recall being called, for the first time, "a dirty Jew." I looked at myself. I had bathed, my clothes were washed and clean, and I wore shoes that were polished until they shone. I looked at the person who called me this and said, "Take a look at yourself in your dirty clothes and worn-out shoes with holes in them. You are calling me dirty?" He looked at himself, said nothing, and ran away.

* * *

Antisemitism, hatred targeting Jews, is often referred to as the world's oldest hatred. This is because violence against Jews, for being Jews, as you will read in the next chapter, has been a recurring theme of Jewish life for three thousand years. Some would say that the Pharaoh, in the Book of Exodus in the Torah, is the first ruler to exhibit violent antisemitism when he feared that the Israelites were becoming too numerous and ordered the killing of all baby boys born to Israelite women. Another effort at the annihilation of the Jews is found in the Book of Esther, occurring in the fifth century BCE. Haman, an official in the Persian court of King Ahasuerus, was so angry when Mordecai, a Jew, refused to bow down to him that he "plotted to do away with all the Jews . . . throughout the kingdom."[1] He told the king, "There is a certain people, scattered and dispersed among the other peoples in all the provinces of your realm, and whose laws are different from those of any other people and who do not obey the king's laws; and it is not in your majesty's interest to tolerate them."[2] So he requested the king to draw up an edict for their "destruction."[3] The Jewish People were saved by the efforts of *Hadassah*, or Esther, but the hateful and dangerous themes involving accusations of difference, disloyalty, and statelessness would persist to the present day.

Before I delve into the details of antisemitism, I want to tell you a little about where the word "semite" comes from in scripture. After the flood, Noah and his descendants were instructed by God to adhere to the seven Noahide laws: establish courts of justice and do not murder, steal, commit adultery, worship idols, blaspheme God, or eat flesh torn from an animal. Tradition tells us that Noah's son Shem took on the responsibility to teach these universal laws by establishing the first university, and the word "semite" comes from Shem's name. In my understanding, a semite is a person who lives by and teaches these universal laws by focusing on the Godliness of every human. In the semitic worldview, all humans have a right to exist, have a relationship with God, and have these rights protected. Under this view, no people, race, or faith is superior. Therefore, an antisemite believes the opposite: that one particular people, race, or faith is superior and should dominate all others. At the root of antisemitism is the rejection of these universal ethics espoused by Jewish tradition.

Over the centuries, we have seen antisemitism take on various forms, nearly all of which are based on lies and conspiracy theories about who the Jewish People are and what they do or believe. Ambassador Deborah Lipstadt, the US Special Envoy for Monitoring and Combating Antisemitism and a renowned scholar on the subject, advises, "It is important [to] understand that antisemitism, as is the case with any prejudice, exists independently of any action by the Jews."[4] She goes on to ask, "Given the absurdity of anti-Semitic accusations, why do they gain any traction? One explanation may be that, having been embedded in society for millennia, they have gained a staying power that is hard to eradicate. Antisemitism also becomes a means of explaining otherwise inexplicable situations."[5] For example, as Holocaust scholar Yehuda Bauer puts it, "Nazi ideology was not rooted in political, economic, or military pragmatism. It was based on pure fantasy, a so-called Jewish conspiracy to control the world. The 17 million Jews who lived in the world before WWII, who couldn't agree on a single thing—not even on who they were—were suddenly transformed into a world conspiracy."[6]

The lies that form the basis of antisemitism, because they have been repeated and reimagined in every age, have become recurring themes, or tropes, that shape-shift to fit the hateful needs of every generation. These tropes include falsehoods based on power, money, greed, and loyalty. Hatred of Jews was also historically a mainstay of the Christian religious tradition, in which Jews were blamed for the death of Jesus Christ, himself a Jew. Lies about Jews and their practices have been a regular feature of the marginalizing and demonizing of Jews and have led to violence against their communities. In addition, Jews have existed as a minority in every community in which they have lived since being exiled from the land of Israel in 70 CE after the destruction of the Second Temple. It is only since the founding of the State of Israel in 1948 that Jews have had a place where they live as the majority group.

Events of the twentieth century have engendered two additional forms of antisemitism: denial that the events of the Holocaust happened and hatred of Jews based on the existence of Israel as a Jewish homeland; in essence, hatred based on Zionism.

To help understand what antisemitism is, the International Holocaust Remembrance Alliance convened scholars in 2015 to develop a framework for a working definition of antisemitism. IHRA is a multinational organization dedicated to remembering the Holocaust and the accompanying genocide of the Roma and working to prevent further genocides. In 2016, it issued the following "non-legally binding working definition of antisemitism":[7]

Antisemitism is a certain perception of Jews, which may be expressed as hatred toward Jews. Rhetorical and physical manifestations of antisemitism are directed toward Jewish or non-Jewish individuals and/or their property, toward Jewish community institutions and religious facilities.[8]

This definition has been adopted and is in use by many organizations and governments, including the United States. IHRA also offers the following helpful examples when considering whether ideas, attitudes, speech, or actions consist of hatred targeting Jews:

Manifestations might include the targeting of the state of Israel, conceived as a Jewish collectivity. However, criticism of Israel similar to that leveled against any other country cannot be regarded as antisemitic. Antisemitism frequently charges Jews with conspiring to harm humanity, and it is often used to blame Jews for "why things go wrong." It is expressed in speech, writing, visual forms and action, and employs sinister stereotypes and negative character traits.

Contemporary examples of antisemitism in public life, the media, schools, the workplace, and in the religious sphere could, taking into account the overall context, include, but are not limited to:

Calling for, aiding, or justifying the killing or harming of Jews in the name of a radical ideology or an extremist view of religion.

Making mendacious, dehumanizing, demonizing, or stereotypical allegations about Jews as such or the power of Jews as a collective—such as, especially but not exclusively, the myth about a world Jewish conspiracy or of Jews controlling the media, economy, government, or other societal institutions.

Accusing Jews as a people of being responsible for real or imagined wrongdoing committed by a single Jewish person or group, or even for acts committed by non-Jews.

Denying the fact, scope, mechanisms (e.g., gas chambers) or intentionality of the genocide of the Jewish people at the hands of National Socialist Germany and its supporters and accomplices during World War II (the Holocaust).

Accusing the Jews as a people, or Israel as a state, of inventing or exaggerating the Holocaust.

Accusing Jewish citizens of being more loyal to Israel, or to the alleged priorities of Jews worldwide, than to the interests of their own nations.

Denying the Jewish people their right to self-determination, e.g., by claiming that the existence of a State of Israel is a racist endeavor.

Applying double standards by requiring of it a behavior not expected or demanded of any other democratic nation.

Using the symbols and images associated with classic antisemitism (e.g., claims of Jews killing Jesus or blood libel) to characterize Israel or Israelis.

Drawing comparisons of contemporary Israeli policy to that of the Nazis.

Holding Jews collectively responsible for actions of the state of Israel.

Antisemitic acts are criminal when they are so defined by law (for example, denial of the Holocaust or distribution of antisemitic materials in some countries).

Criminal acts are antisemitic when the targets of attacks, whether they are people or property—such as buildings, schools, places of worship and cemeteries—are selected because they are, or are perceived to be, Jewish or linked to Jews.

Antisemitic discrimination is the denial to Jews of opportunities or services available to others and is illegal in many countries.[9]

This definition, by executive order, is utilized by the US Department of Education in evaluating antisemitism in schools. It also is the definition incorporated into the United States National Strategy to Counter Antisemitism, issued by the White House in May 2023, and is incorporated into the proposed Antisemitism Awareness Act.[10]

You may wonder how this shows up in real life. Antisemitism based on lies about Jewish power, money, and/or greed or, as the IHRA definition reads, blaming Jews for "when things go wrong," including lies about the Jews "controlling the media, economy, government or other societal institutions," is commonplace and pervasive. Recent data shows that "38 percent of Americans thought Jews always like to be at the head of things, 26 percent thought Jews have too much power in business, and 20 percent thought Jews have too much power in the United States today."[11] The percentage of people harboring similar antisemitic beliefs globally is even higher.[12] This kind of antisemitism is frequently used by both white supremacist and neo-Nazi groups as well as by foreign governments and anti-Israel organizations. These groups and their followers have regularly spread lies that Jews are the "puppet masters" pulling the strings of governments, people, and institutions around the world. One particularly deadly example of this is known as the "Great Replacement Theory." This lie posits that Jews around the world are somehow secretly organizing immigration of Black and Brown people into predominantly white countries, to overwhelm the white communities and take control of them. This lie was shouted at the deadly white supremacist rally in Charlottesville, Virginia, in 2017 ("Jews will not replace us"). People who believe in and espouse this conspiracy theory have been motivated to violence, this includes the shooter at the Tree of Life Synagogue in Pittsburgh, Pennsylvania, who in 2018, murdered 11 Jewish worshipers. Belief in this theory also resulted in deadly mass shootings of Latinos in El Paso, Texas (2019), Muslims in New Zealand (2019), and Black people in Buffalo, New York (2022). This is a reminder that antisemitism is deadly, and its violence is never limited to Jews.

Another "mendacious, dehumanizing, demonizing" series of allegations about Jews that has resulted in much hatred and violence concerns the historical claim that Jews killed Jesus ("decide") and that Jews murder non-Jews for some nefarious ritual purposes ("blood libel"). Both forms of antisemitism have their roots in the Christian religious tradition and have resulted in centuries of violence against Jews. These false beliefs have, sadly, remained prevalent and have taken on modern forms. For example, both white supremacist groups and anti-Israel groups continue to spread propaganda blaming Jews for both killing Jesus and Muslim prophets. This type of antisemitism has recently resurfaced in cartoons and social media posts that "accuse Israel of stealing organs from Palestinians killed in Gaza, [claiming] that 'child murder' was a preferred 'ritual' for Israel, with babies being a 'favorite target.'"[13]

The IHRA definition is also very clear that denying the Holocaust happened or minimizing its effects is antisemitism. Many mistakenly believed that the horrors of the Holocaust would have resulted in a permanent revulsion of antisemitism, but that is not the case. Again, this type of hatred is common among both white supremacist/neo-Nazi groups and anti-Zionist/anti-Israel groups and their supporters. Such a conspiracy theory is very dangerous as it allows humanity to ignore historical facts and makes it harder to prevent such atrocities from happening again, to the Jews and other marginalized groups. Ignorance about this history and the prevalence of such conspiracy theories have seeped into society at large. Voices of Hope (VOH), a Holocaust education organization that I helped to found, says it this way:

Today's students are the last generation who will have the opportunity to meet a Holocaust survivor and experience firsthand testimony. Yet, even now, when we still have the survivors' voices to speak, the world is forgetting. Results of the **Holocaust Knowledge and Awareness Study** commissioned by the Conference on Jewish Material Claims Against Germany were released in September 2020. Some of the findings include:

20% of millennials and Gen Z in New York feel the Jews caused the Holocaust.

48% of millennials and Gen Z could not name a single one of the 40,000 concentration camps or ghettos that existed during the Holocaust.

56% of millennials and Gen Z were unable to identify Auschwitz-Birkenau.

49% of millennials and Gen Z have witnessed Holocaust denial or distortion on social media.

70% of Americans believe fewer people care as much about the Holocaust as they used to.

58% of Americans believe that something like the Holocaust could happen again.[14]

In addition, research shows that belief in conspiracy theories leads to the endorsement of antisemitic ideas. For example,

those who embraced conspiratorial ideas like the Great Replacement Theory, were inclined to endorse more antisemitic ideas, which often take the form of a conspiracy theory about alleged Jewish power and subterfuge. . . . Holocaust denialism and distortion often include elements of conspiracism, frequently based in the fantasy that Jews invented or exaggerated the Holocaust as part of some nefarious agenda.[15]

This information evidences the importance of addressing the antisemitism of Holocaust denial and emphasizes the need for more effective education on this topic.

The IHRA definition is very clear that criticism of "Israel similar to that leveled against any other country" is not antisemitic. We can criticize decisions and actions of the Israeli government in the same way that we are free to criticize the actions and policies of our own government. The last seven examples contained in the IHRA definition concern attitudes and ideas around Israel that are antisemitic. Sadly, we are seeing far too many of these. Recent data shows that "39 percent of Americans thought Jews are more loyal to Israel than to the United States."[16] In addition, foreign terrorist organizations are openly antisemitic. For example, the charter of Hamas, the terrorist organization responsible for the attacks on civilians in Israel on October 7, 2023 (and many others over the years), calls for the "obliteration" of Israel in Hamas' "struggle against the Jews." It considers all of the State of Israel "Moslem land" with no place for Jews, asserts that Jews and Christians must acknowledge the superiority of Islam and equates the behavior of Jews in Israel with that of the Nazis. The charter also states that "Judgment Day" will not come until the Jews are killed and encourages its followers to make this happen.[17] All of this is virulently antisemitic and hateful and is mirrored by nearly all radical Islamist organizations and by the governments and education systems of several Muslim-majority countries. In a world where there are only about 16 million Jews (0.2 percent of the world's population) and there are 2 billion Muslims and nearly 50 countries that have a majority population of Muslims, this type of antisemitism is an ongoing and growing concern.

I also want to mention a type of hate that I experienced during the Holocaust which I call "racial antisemitism." We must never forget that the seeds of the eventual Holocaust began with words and ideas in which Jews were considered to be a race that was subhuman, well below the white Aryan race. This idea then mushroomed into sinister cartoons and stereotypes and, a few short years later, became codified into the Nuremberg Laws of 1935.[18] These laws, among other things, outlined who was to be considered a Jew. Jews of the "first degree" were those with at least three Jewish grandparents and "half Jews" were those from a mixed marriage. In many, if not most, circumstances they were treated as one and the same. The goal of the Nazis was to make Germany, then all of Europe and eventually the world, "*Judenfrei*" or free of Jews. For the most part, it didn't make a difference whether a person lived or even identified as a Jew—the extermination order applied to whomever the Nazis deemed as such. This idea of Jews as a distinct non-white race was widespread in Europe and the United States and persists among antisemites to this day. It is another example of the interconnection between antisemitism and other forms of hate, such as anti-Black racism. It is also important to understand, as you will see in later chapters, that the Jewish People are diverse in every way and come in every color of humanity. Indeed, fully half of Israeli Jews and between 12 and 15 percent of American Jews identify as people of color and these numbers are growing.

The Anti-Defamation League (ADL), an organization founded in 1913 to "stop the defamation of the Jewish people and secure justice and fair treatment to all," has been collecting and auditing data on antisemitic incidents, both in the United States and globally, since 1979.[19] Recorded incidents include verbal attacks in schools and other public places; the spreading of hateful propaganda via leaflets, stickers, and other means; bomb threats, swatting, and doxing; vandalism; harassment; and assault and other acts of violence toward the Jewish People and their institutions. Ten years ago, in 2014, ADL recorded just under one thousand such incidents in the United States. Three years later, in 2017, the number of incidents had nearly doubled, an alarming rise in expressions of anti-Jewish hate. Over the next six years, the rate of hate incidents nearly doubled again to over 3,600 incidents in 2022. From October 2023 to October 2024, incidents exploded to over 10,000.[20] These incidents included thousands of cases of harassment, nearly two thousand incidents of vandalism, and over 150 physical assaults. Incidents reported on college campuses increased by a shocking 500 percent in one year. Antisemitic attitudes are also increasing. Recent research shows that 20 percent of Americans hold six or more antisemitic beliefs. The data on incidents and attitudes for the United States shows a steady and alarming year-over-year increase in anti-Jewish hate that shows no sign of abating and is mirrored in data collected globally. It is especially disturbing that recent data shows that younger generations endorse more anti-Jewish tropes.[21] In 2024, Jews were attacked by mobs in the streets of Amsterdam and Berlin, and the authorities in Berlin have told Jews and members of the LGBTQ community to avoid certain neighborhoods of the city because their safety cannot be guaranteed.[22]

I have seen where hateful words, attitudes, and actions against the Jews can lead. I lived through the Nazi murder of eleven million people. Six million of them were Jews; the rest were dehumanized and dispensed with for other reasons having to do with their identities, disabilities, or political views. Some people are annoyed when the Jewish community vociferously calls attention to antisemitic words and attitudes, in the same way that some complain about Black people calling out racism, but if we do not shout about this when we see it, how will we be able to stop it before it evolves into something even more deadly?

As you know by now, I am ninety-five years old. I do not play video games, and I do not spend time on social media. However, I am well aware that antisemitism and other forms of hate are widespread online in both of these arenas. I have learned that hundreds of millions of people use platforms to play online games and that hate is out of control in these spaces, including virulently extreme white supremacist images and ideology, along with glorification and support for terrorist organizations. Many parents are unaware that their children are regularly exposed to hateful content through gaming.[23] In addition, social media is rife with extremist, hateful content, including unhinged conspiracy theories blaming the Jews for every ill in the world.[24] Unfortunately, the reach of the internet is limitless, which means that false and extremist material can infect more minds than we have ever seen in our history.

Sometimes people ask me, who are these antisemites, these haters, and why do they believe these lies? I think the main thing is that people find it easier to hate someone they perceive as different from themselves. Humans are tribal animals; we form ourselves into groups. We find it naturally easier to be altruistic toward those with whom we are related and with whom we share other similarities. But the opposite can also be true—toward the stranger, we feel fear, and that fear is capable of turning us into monsters. Even the most universalistic of religions, founded in scripture espousing principles of love and compassion, can view those outside their faith as Satan, the infidel, the antichrist, the unredeemed, and, therefore, undeserving of empathy and protection. This natural fear of difference can be, and has been, manipulated by leaders through the centuries to dehumanize others who believe, act, look, or love differently.

Sometimes people who fall prey to antisemitism and hate are angry. Maybe they feel a deep emptiness inside or a lack of self-worth, and maybe that makes them explode with envy and anger at people who are different and whom they perceive to have one advantage or another. This jealousy and envy can engender feelings of not belonging that can be exploited by those seeking to recruit more haters to their cause. Sometimes self-loathing plays a role and causes people to lash out—they try to make themselves appear better by detracting from others. One seems innocent in their own eyes by accusing others of graver faults.

Whatever the reason that people are drawn to hate, we must never forget the depths of degradation to which evil can descend. We must be concerned whenever and wherever these evils rear their ugly heads. We must do everything in our power to resist them, for they are the breeding grounds for destruction and death. We must never again remain silent when we are witnesses to inhumanity wherever it occurs. When we see antisemitism and hate, we must act immediately and decisively because if we fail to do so, it can metastasize into monstrous dimensions and become even more difficult to stop, as we learned from the Holocaust. When we say never again, never is now.

Jewish teaching views all humankind as created in God's image. This means that there is a reflection of God that is innate in every human being and that every human being has Godly value. This Godliness dignifies all humanity. We must, therefore, recognize each other's right to peaceful existence. Knowledge and compassion are our greatest tools in combating hate. So, let us now delve into some of the lessons I have learned over nearly a century of speaking out and pursuing peace.

2

Understanding the Long History of Antisemitism

In every generation, the lessons of history call us to remember. As we navigate the complexities of modern society, understanding the long history of antisemitism becomes a crucial tool in preventing its resurgence. Through personal stories and scriptural wisdom, we recognize our responsibility: to learn from the past and ensure it never repeats itself. As President Joseph Biden wrote to me in 2021, "Your resilience and ability to turn pain into purpose are inspiring . . . only by acknowledging the truth can we prevent the repetition of atrocities."

* * *

By late spring of 1942, the Nazis had already burned my family's home, belongings, and businesses. They had already rounded up all the Jews of our area into a ghetto in Zhetel, a terrible culmination of their relentless campaign against us. Now they began the process of removing all the Jews for the purpose of killing those who were not useful to them and enslaving those who were.

In a dusty, oppressive space, my family created a hiding place beneath the floor of our small dwelling in the ghetto. Upon hearing that the Nazis were coming, we once again, entered this secret, small space. After five long days cloaked in the suffocating silence of darkness, we were discovered by local villagers looting our home. The sun blazed down upon me, blinding me after so many days spent in hiding. When my grandfather emerged from our hiding place, the villagers began beating him. In his weakened condition, he soon died. The commotion attracted three Nazis. My mother, her eyes filled with fear and love, whispered, "If you can save yourself, try, because this looks like the end." My brother Abraham attempted to run and was shot in the back. Rachmil, my other brother, managed to escape, hiding in the filth of the outhouse. In that moment of chaos, the instinct to survive surged within me. While they were searching our house and interrogating my mother about any valuables we may have had, I snuck away and found refuge under a small bush in the garden with my face buried in the earth. I could hear every terrifying sound around me. They took my mother and my two other siblings away, and so, alone, I began to search for my father.

As I approached the place where he worked, a huge dog began to bark ferociously, attracting the attention of the Nazis. Suddenly, I was apprehended.

They brought me to the Kino, a movie theater in Zhetel, where the rest of the Jews from the roundup awaited their fate. As I wove through the throngs of people, I discovered my mother and my two younger siblings, Aaron and Rachel! I was so relieved to see them that I embraced and held tight to them.

The theater was large and dark, and we found space on the second floor, along with many other Jews. The windows had been covered with thin wood, allowing only a few rays of sunlight to filter through the cracks. There was enough light for us to see the guards and their rifles with their ugly bayonets. One guard passed nearby, and I could see his face was contorted by an expression that seemed to combine anger and guilt, bitterness and aversion.

There were already a few hundred people in the theater, with more continuously arriving. Every hour Jews who were found hidden away or struggling along the highway trying to make it to another ghetto were captured and added to the already crowded theater. There was no room to move and little air to breathe. A strange numbness settled on us; we were shrouded in a heavy blanket of gloom.

The theater was hot. The air was foul from the large number of frightened bodies crammed together. There were no toilets. There was not even room to lie down; people had to stand. Anyone who could manage to lie down had to lie in filth and excrement. I saw people losing their minds. There was no water. Some of the people in the theater consoled themselves by believing that they would be saved and sent to work, but this never happened.

We all knew what tomorrow would bring, but in what form would our anticipated death arrive? Bullets? Fire? The Nazis were fond of jamming Jews into buildings, especially synagogues, and setting the structures ablaze, efficiently killing everyone inside. Or would it be a trip to one of the death camps we had heard of? These thoughts were coursing through everyone's minds, and some stood motionless while others became disoriented. Some tried to speak but could not. It was a new kind of hell.

In the morning, we were given a bit of dry bread. We heard the name Lazowski called. To our surprise, father's employer was there with a package of food, along with a note that said father was alive. It was another strange quirk of the Nazi mentality that people jammed in the theater were allowed to receive packages. Father had learned we had been caught in Judenrein—"Jewish cleanup." His boss had kindly brought the package to us. Mother sent back a message that father should not come to the theater, but he or his employer should still try to help us if possible.

After receiving the package, we inched toward a window in the back of the theater, hoping to get some air. We found a fairly good spot, but mother did not want to stay there. Father's employer had told her he knew a policeman well and would see if he could help us. Mother was afraid we would miss the policeman if he came, so she asked a woman to inform us if anyone came looking for her.

A policeman did come, but the woman my mother had spoken with told him she had never heard the name Lazowski. He left, taking any hope we had with him. When we saw her later, that woman told my mother that she didn't know where to find us when the policeman came. Perhaps in the grip of terror, she could not recall my mother's words.

Time passed slowly; it was agonizing. After two days of being locked in the theater, we heard trucks pull up in front. Trucks meant death—we all knew this. A Nazi dressed in that fateful, yellow Schutzstaffel, or SS, uniform appeared and began arbitrarily smashing people in the face with the butt of his rifle and sending them out of the theater.

"Mother let's not be first," I said, taking hold of her, Rachel, and Aaron. We began moving toward the back of the second floor, settling near a window covered with thin boards. From here, we could see the crowd of Jews in the theater becoming thinner as the Nazis beat them and sent them outside. The window next to us was high up, and at only eleven years old, I was so small that I could not reach its sill. My mother found a broken chair in the corner and held it as I climbed on it and peered between the boards to witness another barbaric scene. Jews were being packed into trucks, jammed in like herring in a barrel, screaming so loudly, so painfully, that even some of the Nazi guards averted their eyes so as not to see the distress they were causing. I climbed down and told my mother what I saw.

My saintly mother took the chair and used it to smash the wooden boards covering the window, admitting a flood of sunshine. This light was so powerful, it energized me in a way I had never before felt—this window was the possibility of escape.

"Let's jump, Mother!"

"No, son, I can't. Not with the baby. But I want you to live. You must jump."

I looked at her eyes. Their light spoke of forbearance and mercy. Despite everything, they were still shining with the brightness and strength derived from her faith. I held her tightly and kissed her, saying "I'm not jumping without you."

The Nazi in the SS uniform was back again. Another truck was loaded. He was coming closer and closer to us as the theater emptied. Mother made me climb up on the sill of the window, but I would not, could not jump—not without my family.

"Jump," Mother pleaded. "I want you to live. I want you to tell the world what is happening here. I want you to be somebody. The world will someday need you. My son, may God show you the way."

These were her last words to me.

I stood there hesitating, paralyzed. This was the most agonizing moment in my life; I knew I was about to lose my mother, my brother, and my sister. I was frightened and filled with dread. How could I live without my mother? I would be lost. How would I survive? I didn't want to leave. I was at a standstill. Suddenly, she pushed me out, sending me down two stories into a patch of high grass. A German standing nearby seemed to make a half turn and look in my direction. He was so absorbed in the trucks being loaded that his quick glance may not have permitted him the chance to see me. Or maybe he saw me and chose to say nothing. I do not know.

I looked up at the window. Mother was standing there watching me, and I motioned for her to jump, but she shook her head no. I kept looking at the window. She motioned for me to get away as fast as I could, but I could not take my eyes off her. Suddenly, another boy, even younger than I, jumped from the same window, landing right near me. I looked back at the window. I saw my mother standing there crying, and then she was gone.

* * *

Even though it is painful for me to remember this time, I tell this story frequently. Of course, it is important to me because it was the last time that I saw my beloved mother, brother, and sister. But this moment is also significant because of what my mother told me as she pushed me out the window of that theater. She taught me that memory is an act of resistance. As my mother positioned me for escape, she entrusted me with the weight of our history. Her words, "be somebody," reverberated in my mind, steering my path and purpose. I was her witness, burdened with the call to share our truth. The important lessons I learned through our Jewish faith—about remembering our past, our purpose, and our resilience—echoed deeply in her final plea.

She understood when she charged me to "tell the world what is happening here," that I was a witness to history and that I had a duty to tell people about what I experienced. I don't know whether my mother was familiar with the work of philosopher George Santayana, but she understood that those who do not know history are doomed to repeat it. This duty, to tell what happened, influenced my entire life, and I have carried with me the importance of understanding and studying history so that we learn how to avoid repeating atrocities like the Holocaust.

I believe that being a Jew instilled in my mother the importance of history and retelling the stories from the past. Our faith is built on remembering those who came before us, their stories, and the difficulties that they overcame. We are told in the Torah, "Remember the days of old; consider the years of many generations."[1] Accordingly, many of our holidays celebrate our People's resilience in the face of genocidal regimes. On Passover, we are commanded, "This day shall be to you a memorial; and you shall keep it as a feast to the Lord throughout your generations."[2] So every year for millennia, we recount the story of freeing the enslaved Israelites from bondage in biblical Egypt 3,300 years ago. On Purim, we celebrate the deliverance of the Jewish People in Persia from the murderous Haman, due to the intervention of Esther in the fifth century BCE. On Hanukkah, we celebrate the history of the rededication of the Temple in Jerusalem after surviving an attempted ethnic cleansing by an ancient Greek power, the Seleucids, in the second century BCE. On *Tisha B'Av*, we hear the story of the destruction of our Holy Temple in Jerusalem and our enforced exile by the Romans in 70 CE. Because these rituals were a part of my mother's life and faith, she understood the power of remembering and knowing the past through the telling of these stories every year. She recognized that what was happening to her, my family, and all Jews in Europe during the

Holocaust was the unfolding of current Jewish history and, therefore, needed to be told, again and again.

She was right. And I have told my story countless times. But it is also important to understand the history that preceded the Holocaust so that no one makes the mistake of thinking that it was a random event of great evil and that it couldn't possibly happen again. We need to know, learn from, and remember the long history of the persecution of the Jewish People, including the Holocaust, to prevent such atrocities from happening again.

The past is part of our identity. I believe that if we forget our past, we lose our identity and sense of direction. Not only are those who do not know the past in danger of repeating it, but those who are ignorant of their history will have their history written for them by others.

There are many good reasons to study history: to gain a better understanding of the past; by understanding the past, we can understand the present; and history educates and helps us to know what questions to ask, and by asking questions, we learn. The Holocaust, while on a scale unseen before, did not arise out of thin air. Rather, it was the apotheosis of millennia of virulent and deadly antisemitism, driven by an ideology that sought the worldwide extermination of the Jewish People. For example, the First Temple in Jerusalem was destroyed in 586 BCE by the Babylonians, who forced the Jews out of the land of Israel and into exile. The Temple was the symbol of unity; it was the central address for the spirituality of the Jewish nation. The destruction of the Temple and the forced exile resulted in the loss of country, nationhood, land, people, independence, economic stability, and political rights for the Jews. This would have been enough to overwhelm even the most powerful nations on earth, but the Jewish People survived.

Over five hundred years later the Second Temple in Jerusalem was also destroyed. This time it was by the Roman army led by the future emperor Titus. Jews were massacred and the ancient historian, Josephus, writes that blood flowed through the streets of Jerusalem. When Titus returned to Rome, a triumphal arch was built in his honor. To commemorate that victory, coins were minted with the inscription, "*Judea Capta.*"

However, out of the smoking ruins of the Temple in Jerusalem grew a determination to live and carry on the work of God, "*Lo amut ki-ech-ye*"—I shall not die but live and declare the works of the Lord.[3] This was the battle cry of the Jewish People through the ages. This tragedy resulted in the exile and dispersal of many Jews, but we never abandoned our homeland. Jews fled to Europe (referred to as Ashkenazi Jews), Spain and northern Africa (Sephardic Jews), the Middle East (Mizrahi Jews); the far east (Bene Israel) and Africa (Beta Israel) and later to the western hemisphere. Dispersed, we wandered from land to land, meeting hostility in every corner of the earth.

Around the end of the first century CE, as Jerusalem lay in ruins and anti-Jewish decrees made by the Roman government put severe pressure on the Jews remaining in Judea, the Midrash reports that three prominent rabbis, Rabban Gamliel, Rabbi Eliezer, and Rabbi Yehoshua, traveled to Rome to lobby the Senate on behalf of the Jewish People. The rabbis arrived in Rome, and their mission seemed to fail. They were told that Rome sought the destruction of the Jewish community throughout the Empire. Rome, like Haman in Persia centuries earlier, also planned to exterminate the Jews. We are here as evidence that the Roman version of the "Final Solution" also failed.

The violent and murderous destruction of the First and Second Temples and the resulting exile of the Jewish People are remembered on *Tisha B'Av*, the saddest day on the Jewish calendar. There is an apocryphal story of Napoleon in the streets of Paris on *Tisha B'Av* hearing mournful cries coming from a synagogue. He asked his companions what was happening, only to be told that the Jews were mourning the loss of their Temple 1,700 years ago. Napoleon is said to have observed, "A nation that has mourned its Temple for 1700 years will surely merit seeing it being rebuilt one day." This tale, whether it truly happened, is a recognition of the resilience of the Jewish People.

Tradition tells us that over the past 3,500 years, many of the most horrific events perpetrated against the Jewish People occurred on *Tisha B'Av*. This is another way our tradition calls on us to learn and remember our history. What follows are some of the tragedies that we remember on *Tisha B'Av*.

The fall of Betar and the end of the Bar Kochba Revolt against the Romans occurred in 135 CE. It is estimated that a half million Jews, or more, were killed by the Romans in this revolt, an early example of what the Nazis would later attempt to do with their policy of making Germany "Judenrein." The Romans, who made several similar attempts to eradicate all Jews, were never completely successful. Jews, sometimes only a small remnant, have continuously lived and worshiped in the Holy Land from biblical times.

It is also said that it was on *Tisha B'Av* that Pope Urban II at the end of the eleventh century CE declared the First Crusade to conquer the "Holy Land" from the Muslims who controlled it at the time. During the crusades, tens of thousands of Jews were killed in Europe and in the Holy Land, with many Jewish communities being completely obliterated, simply for the crime of being Jewish.

It is also said that many expulsions occurred on *Tisha B'Av*. The Jews were expelled from England in 1290. As with all expulsions, they could not bring their homes, businesses, and belongings with them. These were stolen by locals just as, hundreds of years later, I witnessed the townspeople of Zhetel take the belongings of the Jews seized and murdered by the Nazis. Jews were not allowed back into England for more than 350 years. Even then, it is hard to imagine that they were welcomed back with open arms. In fact, two hundred years after they were readmitted, a man of Jewish heritage, Benjamin Disraeli, became prime minister. It is reported that he was baptized, possibly in recognition of the societal advantages Christianity would bestow upon him. However, Queen Victoria questioned whether he was really a "full-fledged Christian" and wondered whether he had truly severed ties with his "own people." In response, he is said to have told her he was "the blank page" which separates the Hebrew Bible from the Christian Bible.[4] Despite assimilating and rising to the height of British power, his background and loyalty were still questioned, in classic antisemitic fashion.

In Spain, Jews were expelled in 1492 unless they converted to Christianity. During the Inquisition, countless suspected secret, or hidden, Jews were tortured, and many were killed. Expulsion from Portugal would follow in 1496. Jews were not allowed back into Spain until 1868 and could not openly practice their faith as a community until 1968, well after the Holocaust. Portugal accepted Jews back around 1800.

The Jews were expelled from France and other parts of Europe as well. It is important to remember that each expulsion came not only with the seizure of Jewish assets, property, and businesses, leaving the expelled community impoverished, but each subsequent expulsion reduced the number of places where Jews were permitted to live, causing enduring public humiliation and hardship.

The earliest example of a European blood libel began in England in 1144.[5] It is a lie that asserts that Jews murder non-Jews, especially Christian children, to use their blood for Passover matzah or other ritual purpose. Complex and deliberate lies fed trumped-up accusations and were used to scapegoat and murder Jews in many countries. Nothing seemed to be able to erase from the minds of medieval and later Christians this image of the Jew as a "drinker of blood." The blood libel has shape-shifted over time in various ways that blame Jews for tragedies that befall non-Jews. In 1928, the blood libel reared its ugly head in New York State when Jews were accused in the disappearance of a Christian child.[6] In 1946, two years after the Holocaust, surviving Jews in Kielce, Poland, were accused of a blood libel that resulted in the deaths of more than forty Jews.[7] I recently heard from a Jewish mother that her ten-year-old son was asked by a classmate whether he used blood to make matzah. Today, the blood libel is seen in false claims that Jews in Israel harvest organs of Palestinians.[8]

This ongoing scapegoating of Jews has its roots in many places, including Christian history and liturgy, envy of any success that Jews may have had, ignorance, the desire to blame someone or a group, and manipulation by rulers and authorities.

The First World War began around *Tisha B'Av* in 1914, the resolution of which, agreed upon at the Treaty of Versailles, set the stage for German resentment, the Second World War, and the Holocaust. The long European history of blaming, dehumanizing, scapegoating, expelling, and murdering Jews made us a natural target. European governments, monarchies, churches, and citizens had been marginalizing the Jewish community and blaming us for all life's ills for as long as people could remember, so it was easy to blame us for the problems resulting from the agreements terminating the First World War. Jewish thinker Ahad Ha'am, in his poem from 1892, worried that being exposed to antisemitism for so long could cause Jews to internalize these hateful ideas.[9] Ibram X. Kendi raises the same idea as it relates to the internalization of anti-Black racism in America.[10] This is yet another example of why understanding history is so important.

Tisha B'Av allows us to give expression to the grief we Jews feel over the tragedies, calamities, and suffering experienced by our People over three millennia. On this day, we mourn the losses and the centuries filled with homelessness, murder, persecution, and intolerance. It also allows us to place the Holocaust in a historical arc, showing us the centuries of warning signs leading to evil of great magnitude.

It would be unusual to find another group of people with this kind of annual day on their calendar. Most people attempt to forget and repress or even recharacterize their defeats. We, however, remember our losses on *Tisha B'Av*, not in a spirit of vengeance, but rather in contrition, self-examination, and hope for the future. The tragedies of the ages are not recalled in bitterness, but rather with the inspiration provided by the heroism and self-sacrifice of our ancestors in their great love for and steadfast loyalty to the Jewish People, their faith, and their heritage. *Tisha B'Av* helps us to revere more deeply our tradition for which so much has been sacrificed.

This day also reminds us of the suffering and intolerance that Jews have endured throughout history and across the globe. Commemorating, acknowledging, and learning from the antisemitism that has permeated Jewish history is an important part of *Tisha B'Av*. Knowing our history is something that is embedded in our faith and its practice. Now we must use that knowledge to do as my mother exhorted me to do—tell the world what happened. Understanding, by both Jews and non-Jews, of this long history of antisemitism, is essential to preventing its recurrence. We must learn from this history and commit to treating all humans with dignity and working to prevent hatred.

Beyond *Tisha B'Av*/Europe

The events remembered on *Tisha B'Av* are not the only examples of virulent antisemitism in history. Between the medieval period and the nineteenth century CE, the counter-reformation in the Catholic world renewed and increased anti-Jewish legislation and saw the introduction of the ghetto system (first in Italy and later throughout Europe), whereby Jews were forced to live only in a proscribed area and were locked inside during certain hours.[11] Many early Protestants followed the antisemitism of Martin Luther.[12]

In the nineteenth century, the religious foundations of Christian Europe as well as the monarchy were weakened, and power in Europe shifted toward republican governments and parliaments and away from the church and royal families (the exception to this was Czarist Russia). Yet European churches continued to periodically press antisemitic policies. In the secular sphere, antisemitism took on a new form. It now became supported by racist theories and was used as an instrument of power by political parties. To be sure, religious distrust of the Jews was deeply ingrained in the population and remained a factor. Jews had been persecuted through the ages for professing adherence to a religion that was different from the officially sanctioned one in whatever country they found themselves. Jews had also shown throughout history that they were not prepared to surrender their faith, even under penalty of death. Religious superstitions had thrived in the Middle Ages and persisted in the nineteenth century, an era of industrialization, enlightenment, and national liberation.

The insistence of the Jews on their unique religious observances never failed to arouse fear and distrust among Christians, who were still inclined to look upon the Jews as deniers of the true faith. This attitude was reflected sharply in the Mortara case in 1858.[13] It involved a Jewish child born in Bologna who, at the age of one, became desperately ill and was secretly baptized by his Catholic nurse so he would not die a heathen. He survived, and seven years later the nurse divulged the baptism. The papal authority immediately kidnapped the child, ordered that he be educated as a Christian, and be granted all the privileges of Christian citizenship. Despite the pressure placed on the pope by most foreign governments, including Catholic ones, that the child be returned to his parents, he rejected the request. Prominent American and British Jews attempted to intervene and were unsuccessful. Mortara grew up, entered the church, and died as a missionary priest in Belgium.

Such was the ambivalent climate of the nineteenth century, an era that gave some Jews much longed-for liberty, the opportunity to finally become citizens in many of the countries in which they lived, and to participate more fully in social, political, and economic life, but in which antisemitism persisted. This allowed some Jews to assimilate into the larger society, and sometimes to forget the differences and deep-seated prejudices that centuries of expulsion, exile, and hostility had fostered in the minds of those around them. The Jews plunged with energy, enthusiasm, and the will to succeed into every field opened to them: commerce, industry, the professions, journalism, science, and the arts. Within a generation in Germany and elsewhere, they had moved from a condition of servitude to positions of influence. Excited by the challenges posed to their talents and having little to lose, they were prepared to take risks, in part leading to the rise of the Jewish capitalist. This rapid rise and economic success were bitterly resented, as it had always been throughout history. In 1873, a sudden slump in the German stock market was blamed directly on Jewish financiers, even though very few Jews had been among the speculators. Antisemitic attitudes spread the lie, still in use today, that all financial scandals were of Jewish origin, as part of a supposed vast conspiracy designed to exploit and impoverish white Christian Europe.

Finally, as the concept of nationalism gathered strength and appeal in the late nineteenth century, Jews were increasingly singled out as an "international people," identified and grouped together by a religion, history, shared ancestry, a language, and a body of writing but without their own country. Jews were seen by antisemites to be disloyal to their home countries—they were a people without a nation, never safe nor fully accepted in any country in which they lived. This constant fear and the persistence of antisemitic tropes and conspiracy theories made Jews yearn even more for their ancient homeland.

Russia

There were also problems for Jews in Russia at this time. While still a minority, they were far more numerous there than in any other single country. Deadly pogroms are recorded from the mid-1600s onward. Having been given little incentive to assimilate, the Russian Jews suffered from restrictive legislation regarding rights of residence and were ghettoized in the Pale of Settlement. Movement of Jews out of the Pale was highly restricted. Jews living in the Pale were regularly subjected to "pogroms." These were violent attacks on Jews by local non-Jewish communities that included rape; murder of men, women, and children; destruction of property; theft; and even burning of entire villages. The Jews were falsely blamed for all manner of nefarious actions and suffered the terror of these pogroms.

In the early twentieth century, Jews were blamed for communism. These ideas and activities were largely generated at the universities, to which few Jews were admitted. There was, however, a small group of Jewish communists, with Leon Trotsky as their head, who were influenced by the desire of the Russian people to rebel against the Czar. They joined the Revolutionary Party and sought to share in the Bolshevik rise to power in 1917. (Antisemitism played a role in the eventual death of Trotsky, who fled to Mexico and was murdered there.) Jews were accused in some parts of the world of being evil communists and in other parts were accused of being exploitative capitalists. Antisemitism was able to adapt to make the Jew into the bogeyman wherever and whenever it was convenient to do so, regardless of the truth.

The Protocols of the Learned Elders of Zion

In the early 1900s, the Czarist secret police, using the false name of Serge Nilus, published a book entitled *The Protocols of the Learned Elders of Zion*, which purported to be the records from a series of meetings of Jewish leaders describing their plans for world domination.[14] The entire contents of the book were a fabricated lie designed to inflame antisemitism and deflect criticism from Russia's rulers. Despite being thoroughly and completely discredited as entirely fake, *The Protocols* have had a distressing ability to influence millions of people over the past century. After being used by the Czarists to discredit their enemies, the British, Poles, and Americans (promoted by Henry Ford) used it to argue that the Jews were conspiring to destroy white Christian life. During this same time, Arab nations adopted the lies of *The Protocols* to claim that allowing Jews to live in what was then Palestine would further the Jewish efforts at world domination. Of course, Nazi Germany and Stalinist Russia also promoted *The Protocols* to their people to inflame antisemitism and further the scapegoating of Jews. Despite their outright fabrication, *The Protocols* remain a favorite of white supremacists and antisemites around the world and are actively promoted by many nations, including as television shows. They have even been peddled by Muslim student associations at American universities and remain widely circulated in Russia. The Protocols are one of the most dangerous and long-lasting pieces of disinformation ever created, and modern technology has made their dissemination easier than ever.

The Dreyfus Affair

In the late nineteenth century in France, Alfred Dreyfus, a Jewish captain in the French army, was falsely convicted of treason for passing secrets and sentenced to life imprisonment on Devil's Island. It took the efforts of Emile Zola, the novelist, to denounce the acquittal of the guilty man and the conviction of the innocent Dreyfus. Zola accused members of the General Staff of having openly falsified evidence and deliberately destroying an innocent man's life. After serving five years in a prison colony, Dreyfus returned to France, but he was not exonerated until 1906, twelve years after the inception of the case. Dreyfus was reinstated in rank and received the medal of honor, but the entire case was another example of the power of antisemitic lies.

The Holocaust

Antisemitism in Europe continued to grow in the years between the First World War and the Second World War. In Germany during the 1930s, the rights of Jews to participate in every aspect of society were increasingly curtailed. Eventually, in every land controlled by Germany, Jewish life was made impossible.

On January 20, 1942, shortly after the United States entered the Second World War, a conference was held on the future of the Jews at a villa in the Berlin suburb of Wannsee. Germany was at the height of its power, and the Nazi Party leadership convened to discuss and coordinate the implementation of the "final solution" to the "Jewish problem"—the systematic, government-sponsored policy of mass murder of all Jews. The Jewish future was to be the death of 6 million souls. The Holocaust is:

> a unique, unusual, and unprecedented form of genocide. . . . Because it was to lead to the death of every single individual with three or four Jewish grandparents. In other words, the crime for which people were killed was that they had been born. This was the first time that this had happened in history—and hopefully the last—but certainly the first. All the other genocides that we know of (before, during, and after the Nazi regime) were localized; there was a certain area in which the genocide took place. In the case of the Holocaust, Germany intended to conquer the whole world and reach every single Jew. It was a universal, global, and murderous ideology.[15]

As you know by now, this was not the first time Jews had been targeted for who they are, but the idea that it was to reach every single Jew in the world was new and frightening. I will discuss more on the topic of the Holocaust in my chapter on education.

Resistance During the Holocaust

After my mother pushed me out of the theater window, I looked toward the Nazi's trucks but could see little. They were surrounded by Germans and townspeople who laughed and clapped their hands as they watched the grim scene of helpless

Jews being loaded up, heading toward certain death. The observers made unbearable, unrepeatable remarks. These people were shouting as loudly as they could in their glee to be rid of the Jews. It was a disgusting scene to see people enjoying their hatred so openly.

So I asked God, "Show me your way. Tell me where shall I go?" I felt God direct me to go back to the ghetto, so I, along with the small boy who followed me out the window, headed in that direction, keeping out of sight along the way. I knew this boy—his name was Abe Goldstein. He had lived around the corner from us and was only eight years old. My plan was to go back to the ghetto in the hope of finding someone, anyone, still alive. With the boy in tow, I went out to a side street. It was deserted.

When we reached the ghetto, we saw hundreds and hundreds of people who had descended on the empty buildings to take whatever possessions the Jews had been forced to abandon.

As we were crossing another street, a large empty bottle flew past us out of nowhere. It grazed my ear before shattering in the street with a startling crash that was loud enough to bring people to their doors and windows to see two Jews trying to escape—two prizes to curry Nazi favor.

Certain we were going to be caught, I began running as fast as possible, with Abe right behind me. I looked back to see a man chasing us, so I began looking for an open door, someplace to hide, but there was nothing. We ran into a small garden, and the man pursuing us passed by without seeing us. I felt God was guarding us.

We walked back to the ghetto. Mixing into the crowd was our salvation, and nobody could find us. The looters were not looking for Jews; they were looking for anything that they could carry away.

A farmer struggling, with little success, to remove a small sofa was an opportunity.

"May we help you with the sofa?" I asked. My gesture was not meant to be helpful by any means, but this was a safe way for us to get out of the ghetto. It was *our best chance—we would appear to the Germans to be looters, and they were too busy searching for valuables to be bothered with a small sofa.*

"Sure," he replied quickly. I pulled my cap low over my forehead and asked him if there were any Jews left in the ghetto.

"Not anymore," he said, breathing heavily from his efforts. "The only place I know where there are any Jews left now is Dvoretz. There are still some there."

We helped him lug the sofa and everything seemed safe. Then we ran into a Nazi who wanted to check what we had taken. Civilian looters were not allowed to take anything valuable, and fortunately, the farmer had nothing worthwhile, as far as the Nazis were concerned. We were allowed to continue. We were not far out of the ghetto when the farmer wanted to stop for a rest.

"If we stop here, they're liable to take everything from you. Let's go on a bit until we're away from the Germans," I said.

"Alright," said the farmer, revealing his weariness.

We had not gone too far when I saw a sign pointing to Dvoretz. I gave my companion a wink that clearly said, "Let's go. Now's our chance!" We dropped the sofa and made a dash for a cornfield where the high stalks served as excellent cover.

At daybreak, Abe was despondent and bereft of hope. He decided to go back to the ghetto to be killed. His mother and father had been killed, and he had lost his will to live.

He broke loose from me as I shouted, "Don't go! Don't go!" I stood there and didn't move, watching him walk away. Eventually, I saw him slow down and turn his head back to me, still standing there. Lo and behold, he changed his mind, walked back to me, and we continued on, just trying to survive.

We headed toward Dvoretz in search of any living Jews. On the way, we were robbed of our shoes and were forced to continue our journey barefoot. Eventually, we reached Dvoretz. A feeling of panic overtook me as I entered the barbed-wire walls surrounding the ghetto. I thought this would be the end. I felt alone and, on the run, like a fugitive. Then, through another miracle, I found my brother Rachmil.

Life in the Dvoretz ghetto was horrific. No food, no mother, no father, filthy conditions . . . orphans scrambling to stay alive. After a time, good news came—my father was still alive! We learned that he was hiding in the woods. This gave us hope—a new lease on life. Within a few weeks, my uncle came with another man and took us from Dvoretz to the woods where many family groups were struggling to hide and survive the genocidal Nazi machine.

* * *

The story of the Jewish underground during the Holocaust, as I experienced it as a child, is filled with various manifestations of courage and heroism. It is a story of faith, self-sacrifice, and superhuman endurance. The Jews had no chance of victory over the Nazis, and yet we continued to fight; we continued to do anything in our power to sabotage and slow down the enemy. We stretched minutes into days and days into weeks to prolong our existence. We did all we could to deny Hitler his dream of totally wiping us off the face of the earth.

We called on spiritual stamina to suffer the rigors of this unnatural existence in the middle of a horrific genocide. But our brave resistance fighters made contributions to the defeat of Hitler. By 1943, some Jewish Partisan units had acquired a fairly advanced level of organization and were relatively well-armed. They fought back in the spirit of the Maccabees. They acquired ammunition, dynamited railroads, and burned bridges. Women played a role in the Jewish resistance as well, some even assuming military command positions.

We were resilient, and we expressed resistance by a variety of means. Of course, as scholar Yehuda Bauer states, those

who had access to arms (however few and ridiculous these arms may have been in comparison to what the Germans had), felt they had a moral obligation to make a statement against oppression and murder. They did this by fighting physically against the Germans, and by any kind of reaction in-between—from maintaining schools and prayer groups to organizing literary and artistic presentations.. . . . We estimate today that approximately 30,000 Jews participated in partisan fighting in the forests of Eastern Europe against the Germans. . . . Most of them died. It didn't prove to be a major way of rescue, but it made a statement.

He goes on to say that "Jewish *unarmed* active resistance was much more widespread than Jewish armed resistance."[16] He also acknowledges that the emigration of about 300,000 Jewish refugees to then Palestine was an act of resistance because "resistance to the Nazis comprised not only physical opposition but any activity that gave the Jewish people dignity and humanity in the most humiliating and inhumane conditions."[17]

By the grace of God, we survived. I am reminded of this story:

* * *

The Jews were being herded into the ghetto and were told that if they did not run, they would be beaten. An old man, bent and infirm, was leading his grandchild by the hand. As they ran, the child fell and bruised his leg. When he got up, he could only limp along. Fearing that the Nazis would club the boy, the old man placed him on his shoulders and forced himself to keep running.

"What are you doing?" someone asked, "You can hardly run yourself. You are old and weak. How can you carry the child on your shoulders?"

"How wrong you are," replied the old man, "I am not carrying the child, the child is carrying me. Were it not for him, I would not be able to take a single step."

* * *

Just like this weak old man, our resistance showed defiance and sheer heroism, even in the face of the mighty armed machine of the Nazi government.

By the end of the Second World War, 6 million Jews had been murdered by the Nazi regime and its many willing partners. This represented two-thirds of Europe's Jews and more than a third of the world's Jews. This was the pinnacle of antisemitism—multi-year state-sponsored mass murder of the Jewish People. Had the Nazis not been defeated, they were on track to exterminate half of all the Jews in the world in less than ten years. This was the culmination of millennia of antisemitism. We must understand this long history of hatred so that we can work to stop it long before it reaches this level ever again.

The Muslim World

In the Muslim world, antisemitic developments were historically less extreme than in the Roman Empire and Christian Europe. Jews were treated like other infidels, or nonbelievers in Islam, as second-class citizens with fewer rights. But for much of this history, until the twentieth century, Jews did not generally suffer the expulsions and murderous rampages in Muslim-majority countries as they did in Christian Europe.

At the dawn of the Muslim faith, around the seventh century CE, the nascent Muslim community worried about the Jews, but being people of the book (recipients of divine revelation), Jews were treated as *dhimmi*, requiring the payment of a tax in exchange for protection. As the Muslim faith grew, Muslim fundamentalist belief emphasized that dhimmitude should be used to suppress the Jews, to make their existence more difficult and to prevent them from prospering or growing in number. (You may remember that Pharaoh in ancient Egypt was concerned about the very same thing when he ordered all the male children of the ancient Hebrews to be murdered.) Muslim fundamentalists (possibly influenced by Christian antisemitism) painted a picture of the Jews as renouncers and falsifiers of God's truth and killers of his prophets. Our return to the Holy Land in the twentieth century CE and the establishment of the State of Israel in 1948 hardened many Muslim's views of the Jews. The Grand Mufti of Jerusalem, Hajj Amin al-Husayni, went so far as to hold a meeting with Adolf Hitler on November 28, 1941, to express his support for Hitler's anti-Jewish ideology and activities.

Sayyid Qutb, the ideologue behind modern political Islamism, wrote an essay, "Our Struggle with the Jews," in 1950 that was popularized in the 1970s and remains influential to this day. In it, he expresses the following lies about Jews: that we have been confrontational with the Muslim state since the establishment of Medina; that the Muslim community suffers from Jewish conspiracies; that the Jews will not be satisfied until they destroy Islam; and that the Muslim war against the Jews must continue.

While there are many Muslims and Christians who do not harbor antisemitic attitudes and work closely with their Jewish friends and neighbors, it is unfortunate that today radical Islamism can be added to historic Christian antisemitism and white supremacy as a source of hate and conspiracy theories about Jews. Both Islamism and some strains of Christianity have seen Jews as a threat to their respective religions and power and falsely characterized Jews as desiring the destruction and subjugation of both Christians and Muslims.

In the second half of the twentieth century, after the Holocaust and the establishment of the State of Israel by majority consensus of the international community, Jews who lived in many Muslim countries were again forced to leave their homes. In a modern-day expulsion, over 800,000 Jews either fled or were forced from their homes in these countries, echoing medieval Europe. The result today is, again, a victory of sorts for the antisemites—many countries in the Middle East, such as Yemen, Iraq, Syria, Iran, Tunisia, and Morocco, that historically had flourishing Jewish communities are now effectively *Judenrein*. They were able to succeed where Hitler was not. In addition, these Jew-free communities also harbor the highest level of antisemitic attitudes seen anywhere in the world today, with over 70 percent of the population harboring multiple antisemitic attitudes and beliefs in antisemitic conspiracy theories.[18]

There are over a billion and a half Muslims and over two and a half billion Christians in the world today. There are fewer than 16 million Jews who, after such a history, crave to live in peace. Both of the world's other monotheistic religions, which trace their roots to the Jews, have long and deep histories of antisemitic actions, including systemic discrimination, expulsion and forced exile, theft, forced conversion, murder, ethnic cleansing, and genocide.

A History of Marginalization and the Jews' Refusal to Conform

Now you see why antisemitism is known as the oldest hatred; its history is long and dark. The idea that Jews are an alien element and, as such, are potentially harmful to the state goes back millennia. The Torah relates, "A new king arose over Egypt, who did not know Joseph. And he said to his people, 'Look, the Israelite people are much too numerous for us. Let us deal shrewdly with them, so that they may not increase; otherwise in the event of war they may join our enemies.'"[19] This is the first Biblical instance of antisemitism on a large scale. It is noteworthy in that it arises not from the Egyptian people, but from the ruler. It is the king who stirs it up. This has often repeated itself in history. In the Book of Esther, the genocidal Haman says of the Jews, "There is a certain people scattered abroad and dispersed among the people in all the provinces of the kingdom, and their laws are diverse from all people, neither keep they the king's laws therefore it is not for the king's profit to suffer them."[20] This verse contains many traditional aspects of antisemitism: the dispersion, statelessness, and disloyalty of the Jews; the suspicions aroused by their customs; and their refusal to adopt the customs of the lands they lived in, all of which give rise to conspiracy theories about and hatred of the Jews. In later antiquity, much of the hatred of the Jews was based upon the Jewish rejection of paganism. The Jewish refusal to worship images and idols led to a series of clashes with the Hellenistic and Roman authorities.

The Jewish People throughout history have refused to change their beliefs and customs to that of the majority culture, in whatever land they found themselves. Moreover, Jewish religious practice (e.g., marriage, dietary laws, observing the Sabbath) cut them off from social interaction with their neighbors. Jews also needed to live near one another for the proper observance of the Sabbath, mourning, and other religious activities requiring a quorum. Because they did not conform to the majority culture, Jews were seen as different, as a threat to the dominant culture and governing authority. This perceived threat needed to be controlled, and, in many circumstances, Jews were scapegoated by the authorities when they needed to direct the anger or discontent of their populace.

In the Christian world, antisemitism assumed tragic proportions. While there may have been individual Christians who did not harbor antisemitic animus, the church, as a powerful institution, found itself in a particularly hostile position with regard to the religion from which it claimed its descent but which had rejected it. The Christian Church alleged that Jews killed Jesus, with further evidence of their crime being their refusal to accept Jesus as the Messiah. The spread and ultimate political success of Christianity led to the emergence of a doctrine that Jews were hated by God, who had rejected them for their sinfulness and obstinacy. Jews were gradually forced out of every sphere of political influence and deprived of civil and political rights. In due course, the church's attempts to erect barriers between Jew and non-Jew were translated into legislation affecting all aspects of Jewish life. Conversion to Judaism became an offense punishable by death. The movement for the destruction of synagogues and forced conversion of Jews to Christianity was strong from the fifth century on. Exclusion of Jews from economic life was the next objective, and, as previously mentioned, expulsions were common.

Hatred of the Jews was fed by liturgical means and by other (e.g., dramatic) commemorations of the crucifixion of Jesus that were liable to erupt with violence against local Jews during the Easter season.

As author Dara Horn puts it:

Since ancient times, in every place they have ever lived, Jews have represented the frightening prospect of freedom. As long as Jews existed in any society, there was evidence that it in fact wasn't necessary to believe what everyone else believed, that those who disagreed with their neighbors could survive and even flourish against all odds. . . . The existence of Jews in any society is a reminder that freedom is possible.[21]

This idea terrifies tyrants of all kinds and, as we have seen throughout history, generates antisemitic conspiracy theories and hatred that can have deadly consequences.

Honoring My Mother's Last Words to Me

When my mother pushed me out of that window so many years ago, she saved my life. She also commanded me to tell the world what happened to the Jewish People. She probably meant for me to tell what was happening at that time, which we would later call the Holocaust. But to understand that moment, we need to understand the history that came long before the Nazis executed a plan that murdered 6 million Jews.

I saw death, starvation, and torture. I saw human beings treated worse than animals. I experienced the daily fight for a morsel of bread. I never got over the pain of seeing people die. The real pain of losing a loved one never goes away. Our memories sweeten or lessen the bitterness, but the grief is still there.

So, let us learn the lessons of history, lessons etched in the pain and suffering of millions during the Holocaust and for millennia before that. As a survivor, I embody the resilience that triumphed over the darkness of hatred. My presence is a living testimony to the strength of the human spirit and the resilience of the Jewish People. We must know our own history and encourage others to learn about it as well because learning about what drives hate and allows such hate to persist for thousands of years is essential to reducing it and preventing it from reaching the level of the Holocaust. Injustice, prejudice, hatred, and ignorance are the ingredients that produce tyrants and tyranny, inhumanity, and tragedy.

The world today is experiencing a worrying rise in antisemitism, and we must not close our eyes to this reality. At Passover, we retell events from thousands of years ago: the exodus from Egypt, enslavement, torture, plagues, and miracles. And we must also consider the most recent example of deadly antisemitism, the Hamas massacre of October 7, 2023, and the rise in hate that continues. We are again facing a dark evil, one that we hoped we had left behind in the ashes of Europe after the Second World War. As we say at the Passover Seder every year, "In every generation they rise against us to destroy us, but the Holy One, blessed be He, saves us from their power."

The stories of our past carry the wisdom of survival; they compel us to stand against hatred today. We have learned from the past and now must draw courage and inspiration from it. Let us carry forward the lessons of our ancestors—their courage, their suffering, and above all, their resilience. This knowledge isn't meant to evoke despair but to equip us with the understanding that allows us to fight against hatred in all its forms. With a commitment to remembering and learning, we honor the past and protect the future.

3

Knowing the Jewish People

The Jewish People live all around the world. After forced exile, we migrated from the Holy Land to Europe, Asia, Africa, and the Americas. We speak a multitude of languages and come in a wide array of colors. As the Jewish Latina state representative Alma Hernandez of Arizona writes:

> Antisemitism today is not just about overt hate speech or violence against Jews. It also manifests in more insidious ways, such as efforts to delegitimize Israel's right to exist and the denial of our diverse identities. One of the most destructive aspects of modern antisemitism is the assertion that all "Jews are white," thereby ignoring the reality that Jews come from a multitude of racial and ethnic backgrounds. This claim is not only false but also profoundly racist, as it seeks to erase the histories and identities of Jews of color. . . . Labeling all Jews as white or demanding that we all "go back" to Poland or Brooklyn, New York, as extremists routinely do, is inherently racist and antisemitic. It erases the rich diversity in our community and ignores the myriad multicultural and multiethnic experiences that shape Jewish identity. This reductionist view not only distorts the reality of who we are but also serves as a tool for modern antisemites to undermine our right to self-identify and our connection to each other.[1]

There are many wrong assumptions about who is a Jew and many conspiracy theories about Jewish beliefs, practices, and power. One place to start is to understand that Jews are a very diverse group of people with a shared history, a language, an ancient and continuous connection to a homeland, a culture, and a religion. Some of us are born Jews, and some of us become Jews. We are much more than a religion—we are a People.

Janice's Story

I grew up in Hartford and come from a religious and Christian family. Both of my parents passed away when I was a teenager, and this left me responsible for raising my younger siblings. This struggle was hard, and I admit that I provided for my family by whatever means I could. Eventually, I was told about the possibility of obtaining a scholarship to attend Trinity College. I applied, was accepted, and eventually graduated with my degree. I have been involved in community activism ever since, fighting for Black people in Hartford and especially for Black women. I am the cofounder of an advocacy and training organization that helps Black women become effective advocates for themselves, their families, and their communities. Later, I started the first Black woman-owned lobbying firm in the state of Connecticut, and lobbying for a wide variety of clients is my primary profession.

Because I was very active in my community, a friend thought that I should meet Alan, who was also very involved in the community, just in a different way. My friend saw us both as having giving spirits and told me that he thought Alan and I looked at the world in similar ways. The first time we met, Alan and I talked for three hours, mostly about our respective families. It felt as if we had known each other our whole lives. I later learned the Yiddish word bashert, *which means something like fate or destiny, and our meeting felt that way to me, it was meant to be. Alan was the big brother I never had, and I felt like God had given us each other as a gift.*

We continued to speak regularly and, a few months after we first met, Alan invited me to Shabbat dinner with his parents, Rabbi Philip and Ruth Lazowski, at their home. I had met Rabbi before and thought he was a kind, elderly man but did not have much of a feeling for who he was. This dinner was in 2018, and I remember wearing a sweatshirt emblazoned with "Voices of Women of Color" on it. I also remember sitting in the chair reserved for Alan, next to Rabbi, and feeling embarrassed that I had done something wrong, but Rabbi simply said, "Sit, sit." So I did, right next to him, with Alan's wife Marcia on the other side.

I noticed how beautifully the table was set and wondered what the silver cups were for. Alan began reading in Hebrew, which, of course, I couldn't understand, but I noticed I started feeling some type of way. Then everyone began to sing a song in Hebrew that I now know is Shalom Aleichem, which means peace be upon you. It was at this moment that I became overwhelmed with feelings and started crying; it was like firecrackers going off, a sense of profound happiness, like an awakening. It felt so familiar in that moment, even though I didn't know what any of the words meant. It felt like home, like a need I had was being answered. I know that everyone noticed my emotional state, but no one freaked out about it, and I did not feel at all uncomfortable.

Afterward I felt really good, and I thought that maybe my feelings were simply related to missing my parents and reconnecting with that sense of home that I had had before they passed away. The next Friday, Alan called me, "Hey sis, want to come to Shabbat dinner tonight?" I thought to myself, well, it was interesting last week, and the food was good, so I'm in. And, again, the same thing happened. Only this time, I was holding Marica's hand on one side and Rabbi's on the other, and I could not stop the tears. I felt a powerful force of love, some kind of deep connection. This was more than missing my parents.

I wanted to know—what did this mean for me? I went home and Googled "what is Judaism?" The first word that came up was "justice." This really hit me. I am about justice. This is one of the words that has been most important to me and my life, and for it to be the first word I saw felt like a sign.

After that, I started having Shabbat dinner with Rabbi and Mama Ruth every Friday. I asked Alan whether Black people converted to Judaism, and he explained that they do and that some are born Jews too, that all kinds of people are Jews. He suggested that I ask Mama Ruth all my questions, as she used to be a religious school teacher. I asked whether you have to know Hebrew, and he said, "My mom will teach you." Every Shabbat I learned a new word in Hebrew. And the feeling that I had on that first Shabbat never left me. I started to ask a lot of questions and do a lot of learning. It seemed like every time I asked a question, Rabbi would hand me a book to read.

I also started going to services at the Rabbi's synagogue. I have always been aware of when I am the only Black woman in a room, but at services in my very white synagogue, I never felt this way. It didn't feel like my Blackness was a factor. The Rabbi helped me to understand the service, and I kept learning. I connected deeply to the Etz Hayim, a song that is sung as the Torah is returned to the ark, honoring the Torah as a source of wisdom and a path to peace. I knew this was where I was supposed to be.

Then the Covid-19 pandemic began, and being part of a Jewish community, or any community, became a lot harder for everyone. But I kept learning and keeping Shabbat, and I even began keeping kosher, almost without realizing it. We, thankfully, survived the pandemic, and I began going to Rabbi and Ruth's again for Shabbat dinner and regularly attending services. I continued studying on my own. Finally, I asked Rabbi if I could convert. His answer was to give me a book about Jewish traditions. I didn't hear a yes. This pattern continued for almost two years—I read a lot of books. By this time, even though I had not had a conversion or even a process building toward conversion, I felt I was a Jew.

Finally, the Rabbi said it was time. He gave me my Hebrew name, Toviah, which means good, because he said that I am a source of goodness. I cannot explain how much this meant to me, I feel such a deep connection to this name. He directed me to a formal conversion class, which I completed in 2024. In that class, I began to see how varied the Jewish People are, both in the United States, in Israel, and around the world. We come in all colors, genders, orientations, levels of observance, interpretations of the Torah, political persuasions, and more. Jewish people are all different, just as Black people are all different. We are connected by the Torah, our ancient and ongoing connection to the land of Israel, free will, and living with the consequences of our actions.

For my conversion, I went to the mikveh *(a purification ritual bath) and met with the* Bet Din *(three members of the Jewish clergy, like a tribunal). It's hard to describe how I felt afterward. It's almost a sense of lightness. I am grateful that my friends and family have been along this path with me and accept and support the choices and decisions that I have made. I feel that I have a special opportunity to help others understand what it means to be a Jew, especially to people who either hold some kind of stereotype about Jews or have no idea what a Jew is. It is a privilege to be in this role. It was a six year-process for me, and it doesn't take everyone this long, but for me each step along the way was beautiful. When I first met Alan, I thought he was a gift God gave me, the brother that I never had. But I realize now that he was the vehicle to meeting Rabbi and Mama Ruth and finding my spiritual home. I wouldn't change a thing about this journey.*

* * *

Some people are surprised when Janice tells them she is a Jew. There is a stereotype about who is a Jew and what a Jew looks like that is uninformed and inaccurate. There are many Jews around the world like Janice, who came to the faith and community via many different paths. There have also been Jews of many different colors and backgrounds for centuries—Jews have lived in the Middle East, Europe, Asia, and Africa for millennia. Jews have lived in the Americas for generations. It is important to know that Jews are not simply people with a common religious belief; we are a People with a faith, a language (Hebrew), a shared history, ancestry, and a homeland (*Eretz Israel*). Throughout history, most Jews have been connected to each other through God, Torah, and the land of Israel and have been united by a common history and destiny, despite variations in native languages, practices, rituals, concepts, and levels of observance.

The Torah tells us that Abraham was the first to understand that all things are linked to one source of life, and that source, God, demands justice, morality, and compassion. This belief in one God, monotheism, is the bedrock on which Judaism is based. This concept is reiterated every day when we say the "Shema," a foundational prayer that simply states, "Hear O Israel the Lord our God, the Lord is one." This idea of one God later became the basis for Christianity and Islam. These later faiths built on this monotheistic foundation but do not supersede or invalidate the beliefs of the Jewish People.

In the Torah, God made a covenant with Abraham and his descendants and gave them the laws of the Torah and their homeland, *Eretz Israel*, the land of Israel. The Torah tells of the slavery of the Hebrews by the pharaohs of ancient Egypt, and the role God played in their freedom. This freedom led to the development of the Jewish People and their settling in the land of Israel. Jews around the world celebrate this deliverance from slavery to freedom every year during the holiday of Passover. Commemoration of God's redemption of the People from bondage, the revelation He gave them at Sinai (the Torah), and the settling in *Eretz Israel* are foundational aspects of the Jewish People.

The faith of Judaism believes that humans were created in "the image of God," meaning that whereas we are human, we carry within us the Divine spark. Because of this, man must strive to keep his soul pure. When we sully it, wittingly or unwittingly, we must cleanse it of evil through atonement and *mitzvot* (good deeds). This practice is humbling, enriching, and enabling. We must also commit to *tzedakah* (charity) and *tikkun olam* (repairing the world). This is the Jewish way.

The Biblical name for Jews as a People is "Israel" or "Israelites" (in Hebrew, *Yisrael*). The name comes from the Biblical story of Jacob, who, on his way to meet his estranged brother, Esau, is alone by the river at night and, while there, he wrestles with a being, often interpreted as God, who gives him a new name. His old name is replaced by a new name, Israel, which means "one who struggles with God" or one who wrestled "with beings divine and human."[2] What does it mean to wrestle with God? Someone has pointed out that wrestling is a unique combination of hugging and fighting. We sometimes embrace the Divine, and sometimes we struggle with it. This is also what we do with all truly important relationships in our lives.

The word "Jew" is derived from the name in the Torah given to Leah's fourth son, *Yehuda*, or Judah. Leah's reason for naming her fourth son Judah is found in Gen. 29:35: "She conceived again and bore a son and declared, 'This time I will give thanks to the Almighty.' Therefore, she named him Judah." The sages explain that the matriarchs, Sarah, Rebecca, Rachel, and Leah, were prophetesses, and they "knew" that Jacob's four wives would bear twelve sons. It was presumed that each wife would give birth to three sons. When Leah had Judah, her fourth son, she recognized she had received more than "her share" and therefore called him Judah as a way of expressing her gratitude to God, because "Judah" has the same root as "*todah*"—thanks. Thus, within the very name of the Jewish People is the "attitude of gratitude." The name also contains the same root as the four-lettered, unsayable name of God which has been said to mean, among other things, "He shall exalt!" What does it mean to exalt God? To exalt God is to reveal every aspect of His existence—spiritual, moral, and intellectual.

The thanks that Leah expressed show that she internalized the kindness received from God and is a model for us to recognize the blessings in our lives, received from God, another person or an agent of God. She recognized that God loves and values her. Being thankful is a way to begin to appreciate your own value and build self-esteem. In our very name, we Jews express our value to the world by acknowledging that God has given us many gifts, including our history, the Torah, and more, for which we give thanks. Through this name, *Yehudah*, we acknowledge, exalt, and carry with us the many spiritual, intellectual, and moral gifts of God.

One important distinction between Judaism and the later faiths that developed from it, as well as other world religions, is that it rejects the worship of any particular individual and instead focuses on ideas and concepts found in the Torah. Traditionally, Judaism views the Torah as the revealed teaching of God. The study, interpretation, and understanding of the Torah are the soul of Judaism and the foundation of the Jewish religion.

The Torah is the story of our People, its spiritual instruction, and the history of our religious civilization. It also requires us to be responsible and care for each other. The Torah begins with the story of God's creation of our world and all that is in it. It does not begin with a Jew; it begins with the story of humanity and ends with the newly formed nation, the Israelites, having been freed from slavery and set to wander in the desert for forty years, on the precipice of entering Israel, the land promised to Abraham and his descendants.

Many other religions are dependent upon the teachings and spiritual experiences of one individual. Buddha, Confucius, Jesus Christ, and Muhammad are revered and worshiped by their respective faiths. These religions represent final revelations of their teachings through their founders. But, while Judaism learns from the strengths and weaknesses of our ancestors, we do not worship Abraham, Moses, the Prophets, or Rabbis. We assiduously study these stories to learn and apply them to our own lives and to our view of the wider world.

What the Torah means to Judaism is illustrated by the devotion of Jews throughout history to its preservation. During times of persecution, when the study of the Torah was forbidden, rabbis would rather suffer the penalty of death than surrender their privilege of teaching the Torah to their disciples. Learning has long been highly valued by the Jewish People, and we have rightfully been called "the People of the Book." Jewish survival after the destruction of both temples in Jerusalem (in 586 BCE by the Babylonians and in 70 CE by the Romans) and their subsequent exile into the four corners of the earth has been attributed to Jewish devotion to the study of the Torah. Without the physical place of our ancient Holy Temple to practice the laws of the Torah as our ancestors did, the People studied to keep their faith and communities connected to tradition and to each other. I encourage everyone to study the Torah, no matter who you are or how deep your beliefs or practices are. It is accessible to all and is full of wisdom on the nature of the Divine, integrity, ethics, compassion, kindness, governance, faith, human nature, and more. The Torah is our life and the length of our days, and to study the Torah is to attain spiritual joy and happiness.

Being a Jew also means to be connected to the joy and despair of Jewish history. For example, the Arch of Titus in Rome was built after the conquest of Jerusalem by Titus on behalf of the Roman Empire in 70 CE. Depicted on the Arch are the seven-branched menorah, the trumpets, and what appears to be the table for the "showbread," all of which were sacred items used in the ancient Holy Temple by the priests and were looted by the Roman army. The Arch became a symbol of the Jewish Diaspora, Jews living in exile from their homeland around the world. In a later era, Pope Paul IV made it the place of a yearly oath of submission, but Roman Jews refused to walk under it. The menorah depicted on the Arch served as the model for the menorah used as the emblem of the State of Israel. When David Ben Gurion declared the independence of the State of Israel, the Chief Rabbi of Italy gathered the entire Roman Jewish community by the Arch and, in a solemn procession, walked the opposite way, away from the arch to symbolize the Diaspora's return to Jerusalem and Israel. My wife Ruth, also a survivor of the Holocaust, walked in that procession when she was thirteen years old. The Arch of Titus represents a nearly two-thousand-year history of exile, suffering, and loss, along with the faith, resilience, and perseverance of the Jewish People. This history, from biblical times to today, including our very ancient, uninterrupted, and enduring connection to the land of Israel, is an integral part of the Jewish People.

Our history and perseverance are also memorialized in the Torah and other Jewish scriptures. Abraham smashed idols and he persevered. Noah saw a world destroyed by flood, faced a new world, and yet he persevered. Joseph was imprisoned and isolated and was later elevated to become the vice-ruler of ancient Egypt, where he beheld a new world of glory and power. Moses saw his people enslaved and led them to a new world of freedom. Job saw a life of trial, misery, and sorrow and eventually beheld a new world of wealth, peace, and joy. Mordecai saw our People threatened with annihilation in Persia, but he and Esther persevered and saw our People enjoy happiness and tranquillity. Jews deeply understand that our history shows that we must endure adversity with dignity and at times face questions of life and death.

I love being Jewish. It is the best way I know of being human because it embodies being in service to God and humanity while also practicing religious tolerance and respect—we do not actively proselytize or force others to convert. To be a Jew means to care for and be concerned about others; to work to improve ourselves, to treat ourselves and others with respect, appreciation, and dignity; to implant in our hearts the love of the one God and concern for fellow humans; to discover a noble purpose in life; and to strive for justice and honesty in our daily endeavors. We must be mindful of the role we play in our world and act to improve it through *tikkun olam* (repairing the world). While there are many Jews who are very secular and may not even believe in God, they are still Jews and often value these very same qualities. For me, respecting the holiness and the sanctity of the Torah, belonging to a congregation in the community, and observing just laws are essential to my being a Jew.

Ken's Story

I was born in 1951 in Canada to Jewish parents. I say that, but my dad, a Second World War veteran who flew as part of the crew with RAF pilots, when asked if he believed in God simply said, "I believed in the pilots who got me home." In fact, my younger brother Mel was named for one of those pilots. My dad didn't have much use for religion. My mother, on the other hand, came from a long line of Eastern European Orthodox Jews, who fled persecution in the "old country" for the opportunity and perceived safety of the New World. I, myself, didn't start "feeling Jewish" until one of my older cousins became a bar mitzvah. This piqued my interest, and I began attending Hebrew school, which I loved, and going to Shabbat services (without my parents) and studying for my own bar mitzvah. Of course, this pleased my mother who looked forward to this rite of passage; she even purchased tefillin (phylacteries) and a tallit (prayer shawl) for me. However, only a few months before the date of my bar mitzvah, my mother passed away. As a young person, this tragic loss had a profound impact on me, and I found myself better understanding my father's lack of belief. How could a benevolent God take my mother from me? I lost my interest in religion but finished my studies and became a bar mitzvah, as I knew it was what my mother would have wanted.

My mother's death sent our small family into turmoil. We were now living in Philadelphia, and my father, who had to travel to New York for work, left me, at twelve years of age, in charge of my two younger siblings. Eventually, the state got involved and threatened to send us to foster care. A Black woman, who was an incredible human being, saved us. Although we were very poor and my father could not afford to pay her much, she took care of us for a while until we could get our lives in order and move back to Montreal. She was a gift.

Eventually we landed in Queens, New York. My father remarried and my stepmother kept the Jewish part of our lives going. We had all the holidays and lived in a Jewish community. My brothers went to Hebrew school and each had a bar mitzvah. But I was done with religion. I went to college and eventually to law school where a fellow student invited me to attend Rosh Hashanah services at The Emanuel Synagogue. I found that I really enjoyed the rabbi at the time. His name was Rabbi Singer, and I appreciated his intellect and creativity (he was a graduate of NYU Law School and had written a screenplay that became a feature film!). Eventually, this led to an introduction to a "nice Jewish girl," marriage, and the birth of our daughter.

Despite all these blessings, I was still not feeling connected and motivated about Judaism. Then one day in 1997, as part of a program for parents of children in Hebrew school at The Emanuel Synagogue, I heard Rabbi Lazowski speak. This was the first time that I heard his harrowing story of loss, resilience, survival, and faith during the Holocaust. This had a profound effect on me. I thought to myself, "If this man, after all he has experienced, still has faith in God and love for Judaism, then so can I." This literally hit me like a ton of bricks. I realized that I had been looking for something all my life, and here it was right under my nose. I began attending Shabbat services again and really dove into what it means to be a Jew. This led me to an epiphany—my father didn't know the first thing about Judaism, but he taught me what was in the Torah by the way he lived his life, ethically and with chesed or loving-kindness.

The synagogue became very important to me. I started reading the Torah, leading a minyan, and contributing to my community. Eventually, I became a leader in my community and was the synagogue president. I remain close to Rabbi Lazowski. Every year he reads the story of Jonah in the afternoon Yom Kippur service. I hang onto every word, and it has always been awesome. And every year it is more awesome—here is a man who has seen the worst that humanity can show us, he has been fasting for nearly twenty-four hours, he is more than ninety years old, yet he is chanting one of the longest readings of the prophets and giving a dvar on its meaning. He inspires me to see that being a

Jew is a beautiful privilege and that we all come to our faith, understanding, and observance in different ways and at different times.

* * *

Ken's story is a reminder that Jews experience their faith in many ways. The Talmud attempts to state the essence of Judaism (Makkot 23B–24A) when it says that God gave Moses 613 precepts, but that later seers and prophets reduced these to certain basic principles: David to eleven (Ps. 15), Isaiah to six (Isa. 33:15-16), Micah to three (Mic. 6:8), Isaiah, again, to two (Isa. 56:1), and finally Habakkuk to one: "The righteous shall live by his faith" (Hab. 2:4). This would be Judaism's guiding principle, and it can be expressed in many ways. Ken, long before he returned to his faith, was a proud public defender, a role in which he lived up to his Jewish faith by working for those in need, especially those on whom most of the world had turned their backs. His later commitment to his Jewish community helped to reinforce the values that, like his father, are expressed in the way he lives his life.

I believe that the Jewish People also have a purpose, a destiny, and a reason for being. We are a family that is bonded together spiritually, intellectually, and socially, to enrich the quality of human life. We must be sensitive to all human beings in need. We must strive to be tolerant, considerate, willing, and eager to help make this world a better place for all. One small example of this is that, whereas Jews represent less than two-tenths of 1 percent of the world's population, they have been awarded over 22 percent of all Nobel prizes. Jews, through their scholarship, writings, research, and actions, have contributed to the improvement of humanity in ways greater than our numbers would suggest.[3]

Another defining characteristic of Jews is the command to treat strangers with fairness and compassion because, as the Torah states, "Remember, you yourselves were once strangers in the land of Egypt."[4] And "You must not oppress strangers. You know what it feels like to be a stranger, for you yourselves were once strangers in the land of Egypt."[5] When kindness is transmitted to a stranger, it brings happiness to both the receiver and the giver. An example of kindness to strangers is set forth by Abraham. We read of the tender hospitality of Abraham to strangers in Gen. 18:1-8. When he saw three men standing near him, he ran to receive them, bowed to them, and begged them not to pass by him. He offered them personal comfort and a cool spot in the shade to wash their feet. He personally took care of preparing the meal for his guests of honor, giving them relief and comfort. This is a lesson to all about the importance of kindness to strangers. In fact, God commands us, "Thou shalt not take vengeance, nor bear any grudge against the children of thy people, but thou shalt love thy neighbor as thyself."[6] And further, "If a stranger sojourns with thee in your land, ye shall not do him wrong. The stranger that sojourneth with you shall be unto you as the home-born among you, and thou shalt love him as thyself; for ye were strangers in the land of Egypt."[7]

Rabbi Jonathan Sacks wrote about this in his essay, "Healing the Heart of Darkness," in which he tells the story of Dovid Szegedi, a far-right, virulently antisemitic Hungarian politician who discovered in 2012 that his grandparents were Jews who had survived Auschwitz.[8] This discovery utterly changed his life. He left his political party, studied, and became an observant Jew. Rabbi Sacks says, *"What cured him of antisemitism was his role-reversing discovery that he was a Jew."* He was forced to understand what it meant to be the stranger, and this changed his viewpoint.

Rabbi Sacks says this teaching illustrates that "the best way of curing antisemitism is to get people to experience what it feels like to be a Jew" and "the best way of curing hostility to strangers is to remember that we too—from someone else's perspective—are strangers."

Rabbi Sacks also recognizes that in challenging times, it can be very difficult to be compassionate toward the stranger. He states:

The great crimes of humanity have been committed against the stranger, the outsider, the one-not-like-us. Recognizing the humanity of the stranger has been the historic weak point in most cultures. . . . Dehumanize the other and all the moral forces in the world will not save us from evil . . . to love the stranger appears thirty-six times in the Torah. Jewish law is here confronting directly the fact that care for the stranger is not something for which we can rely on our normal moral resources of knowledge, empathy, and rationality. Usually, we can, but under situations of high stress, when we feel our group threatened, we cannot. . . . The problem arises at times of change and disruption when people are anxious and afraid. That is why exceptional defenses are necessary, which is why the Bible speaks of memory and history—things that go to the very heart of our identity. We have to remember that we were once on the other side of the equation. We were once strangers: the oppressed, the victims. Remembering the Jewish past forces us to undergo role reversal. In the midst of freedom we have to remind ourselves of what it feels like to be a slave.[9]

Hand in hand with remembering that we were strangers in an alien land is the exhortation to remember that we were also slaves in that land. This means that it is the Jewish way to understand the marginalized, those in bondage, and those suffering from discrimination. This means to regard another's dignity as sacred as your own.

The Torah teaches us that there are limits on our behavior; we must know that not everything we desire is permissible. This applies not only, for example, to what we eat but also to how we behave. Good relationships flow from good deeds, good habits with your neighbors, and with people in general.

Jews also know from experience that we must often be willing to stand alone against the outrageous attacks of people who want to destroy us or others to gain power, glory, and riches. We must be aware of what is going on in our community, our nation, and in the world, and speak up when necessary. We are obligated to speak out against lies and conspiracy theories, including those told about the Jewish People. We cannot escape or deny our heritage, nor hide our Jewishness. We must be responsible human beings, morally upright in our actions, behavior, and intentions. We must exemplify honesty in business, integrity, self-control, and self-respect. We must strive for a pure heart and clean hands.

In addition to moral uprightness and intellectual integrity, it is an important Jewish value to be of service and give back, combining the ideas of *tzedakah* and *tikkun olam*—charity and repairing the world. We must develop ourselves to our highest and best to be most useful to our community and beyond.

Looking back at nearly 3,000 years of persecution and torture, it feels like a miracle that the Jewish People have survived and thrived. Many empires have risen and fallen: Babylonia, Egypt, Persia, Greece, Rome, and the Jewish People have continued to survive and, in many cases, to thrive. To be a Jew is not easy. It takes courage, vision, responsibility, and hope. I am very grateful to have had the opportunity to impact the lives of people such as Janice and Ken. It is an honor to be able to help people understand and know the Jewish People and to do so in a way that even inspires them to become Jewish or to return to the faith in a process of learning and discovery. This has been a great blessing in my life. Remember that the lessons of the Jewish People are available to anyone—they are universal. Studying the Torah is available to anyone as well, Jews and non-Jews. The better we all understand who the Jewish People are, that they are diverse and live in many countries around the world, and what our texts teach us, the more people will realize that antisemitism is a wrongheaded mistake. I encourage Jews to take pride in their heritage and who they are and to share this with others, and for non-Jews to be curious about us and take the time to learn.

4

The Power of Faith

Faith and prayer have been central to me in surviving antisemitism, fighting hate, and working for a more peaceful world. My experience tells me to believe in God, Judaism, the Jewish People, myself, and others. Faith and prayer help me to persevere and to keep doing the work of *tikkun olam*. True faith equips the believer with the power to see the possible in the impossible, take the sting from every loss, and quench the fire of every pain. It keeps hope alive.

Miriam, Whose Faith Saved My Life

The last sight of my hometown, where generations of my family had been born and raised, was a painful and traumatic moment in my young life. The Nazis had forced all the Jews, whom they had not yet killed, to leave their homes and be confined together in a ghetto in another town known as Zhetl, which was bordered by forests.

The first massacre in Zhetl took place on April 30, 1942 (several weeks before we would be rounded up into the theater). Night had fallen and I couldn't sleep. I heard the sound of trucks and looked out the window. The ghetto was surrounded, and the Nazi machine guns were positioned to kill. No sooner had I warned my mother of what I saw than the machine guns began firing, indiscriminately killing anyone in their path.

By the next morning, they surrounded the ghetto and began shouting, "Raus, raus! Out, out, get out of your houses." All the Jews were commanded to leave their ghetto homes and go to the marketplace. We had heard that the Nazis were killing all the Jews in other ghettos. Now we understood that they had come for us.

We were aware that they were forcing Jews to dig pits near the cemetery. Later, we witnessed the horrifying scene unfold as the Nazis and their local collaborators lined the Jews up along the edge of the pits and executed them, ensuring that their bodies would fall directly into the holes, making the task of burying them all the more efficient.

Fearing such an event, my family, like many others, had prepared a hiding place by creating a cave in the house in which we were confined. As the eldest son (at eleven years old), it was my job to close the hatchway once everyone was hidden inside, and to spread dirt to camouflage the entrance. With everyone hidden and quiet, I had to find a different place to hide. I was afraid, and pain gripped my stomach at the thought of my own death. Then I thought, "So what? At least my family is safe."

Before I had a chance to run and hide, the front door was suddenly smashed open with a thundering crack from a rifle butt. It was a Nazi with an expression of pure fury on his face. He roared his demand to know where my family was. "They've all gone to the marketplace as they were told," I lied. "Why are you here?" he demanded to know. "I forgot my coat," I replied. "Where you're going you don't need a coat. Run, otherwise I will shoot you right here." I ran.

I found myself as part of a procession into a horrible scene. Thousands of Jews with pale faces and frightened hearts stood in the cemetery, waiting to be shot. Cries of agony reached the heavens. The scene was frightening and gruesome. I saw a couple dancing in the midst of the murdered and still others who had lost their minds. I saw a blind man who was butted in the head with a rifle. Suddenly he could see and was terrified. I saw a woman breastfeeding her baby when a Nazi used his bayonet to pierce the baby like a football. We were all Jews, watching the slaughter and waiting for our own turn. The Nazis observing and directing this scene were like untamed animals, with the predatory and murderous instincts of beasts. I could not comprehend how they could be so bloodthirsty and inhumane.

Then the selection began. The Nazis were masters of deception. We were told that we were being sent to work centers, while in reality I knew we were being sent to be killed. Those chosen by the Nazis to live, at least temporarily, were men and women capable of labor that could be of use, primarily doctors, nurses, cobblers, and tailors. They were allowed to take their families with them. Those chosen to die were the elderly, the unwell, pregnant women, and children.

At this point, I realized I had no chance of surviving by myself. My turn in the selection line was rapidly approaching. I realized the end was coming. Thank God my family was not there, but I was a child, only eleven, and I knew no one. I desperately searched the faces to see if there was anyone who might be willing to "adopt" me as a son for the moment. A strange, remote feeling crept over me. I saw clearly that I was going to die. I was utterly alone, and I was staring into the abyss of death. Then suddenly, my imagination grabbed me. I told myself, "Don't give up! Don't get paralyzed! Use your brain!" I thought of Mama's words, "Think of your faith, don't lose hope. Act now."

So I began quietly begging families with children, "Please, take me as your son." But they answered, "We have our own." And still, I thanked them. But I did not give up. I went further into the crowd, where I noticed a kind-looking woman standing with two frightened young girls who held on tightly to their mother. She was holding a certificate in her hand showing that she was a nurse. That meant life. Gently, in an imploring voice, I told her I was alone and asked if she could tell the Nazis that I was her son. She looked at me with compassion and, although terrified, she said, "If you wish to stay with me, you may. If the Germans let me live with two small children, they will let me live with three." I took her hand and held on tightly.

We came closer and closer to the SS man who was deciding our fates. With a wave of his finger, we were sent to the side of the living. I was saved! I quickly asked the lady for her name. She said, "Miriam Rabinowitz." While there are no words that can adequately describe how grateful I was to have merited the privilege of finding a compassionate stranger, I thanked her for performing an act of chesed (loving-kindness) and saving my life. Then we parted ways.

* * *

Miriam Rabinowitz had faith. She embodied the saying that "a righteous person shall live by his faith."[1] She displayed an astonishing depth of faith in the face of the greatest evil. She had faith in doing the right thing, saving a child's life, and even risked the potential murder of her two daughters and herself in the process. She understood the idea expressed by Rabbi Chofetz Chayim of Radin that for those with faith, there are no questions, and for those without faith, there are no answers. There was no question for her of pretending that I was her son; for everyone else in that line, there was no answer to my plea.

I was raised with faith from my earliest memories, and being alone, fearing the wrong decision in a Nazi selection line tested my faith. But my mother's words that leapt to my mind while searching for help—that I should think of my faith—sustained me. I knew that I had to believe that someone would be kind enough to help. Giving up was not an option.

I feel that my belief in Judaism, my fellow Jews, and the words of my mother led me to Miriam, and the few minutes that she and I shared in that selection line showed me the profound power of faith, both hers and mine. Staring into the face of the deadly antisemitism of the Nazi regime, Miriam's faith said, I will not let your evil win, I will save this Jewish child, I believe in love and goodness, and I believe in the future." Her faith gave her the courage to stand up to hate, and it gave me hope.

After the war, an inscription was discovered on a cellar wall in the city of Cologne, where Jews had hidden from the Nazis:

I believe in the sun even when it is not shining,

I believe in love even when not feeling it,

I believe in God even when He is silent.

This was the kind of faith that motivated Miriam to take the risk to save my life.

During the Holocaust, virtually every day, there were new oppressive Nazi edicts full of cruelty, designed to crush the spirit of the trapped Jewish People. We were overwhelmed by the enormity and scope of the merciless Nazi assault. We were imprisoned in ghettos with violence in every direction. Our peaceful Jewish communities were forever shattered. But our faith helped the few of us who survived to make it through. To me, this faith is the critical substance and essence of Jewish survival through the centuries.

In my experience, nothing is more powerful than faith. Throughout my life, my faith has helped me to overcome obstacles, including fighting antisemitism and hate. It is the motivating force that saved my life and has saved countless people through the ages. Our strength and force come from faith in things we cannot see or touch, and it gives us the ability to say, in our darkest hour, that life is good and worth fighting for.

But faith is not easily found; it must be nurtured, it must be developed.

Billy, Whose Faith Helped Him to Live

In the 1960s, during my early years as a rabbi in Connecticut, I was working with one especially bright and talented boy on his bar mitzvah *lessons. His name was Billy, and he came from a kind and intelligent family who were members of my synagogue. His parents were filled with joy in anticipation of their son's coming-of-age ceremony and celebration.*

Then, one chilly gray day in October 1962, I received a devastating phone call from Billy's father. Billy would no longer need to attend his lessons, he told me, because Billy had just been diagnosed with a rare genetic condition. There was no known cure, and Billy's doctors had told the family that the boy had only three months to live.

I hurried over to comfort the family. I felt the weight of emotional pain in my work—the agonizing confrontation with death. When I arrived at the house, my heart was heavy, but my reservoir of faith and spirituality sustained me and gave me the courage to offer the emotional support and spiritual guidance the family needed in such a devastating moment.

"Doctors can heal, but they cannot always predict matters of health. Because death is in God's hands, we must not lose hope. We must pray for faith to sustain us. God does create miracles," I told Billy's parents.

It was an audacious thing to say, as Billy's father was a doctor himself, but I said it without hesitation or regret. I had experienced miracles in my own life many times, when I thought all was lost and I was about to die. The family looked at me in astonishment. To them, I appeared incredibly young and naive. My words were met with a silence that seemed endless.

Finally, someone spoke, "What are you saying Rabbi?"

Before I could answer, I thought of the biblical command to Joshua, "Be strong and of good courage." This admonition lifted me up whenever I faced discouragement, and in that moment, I felt a surge of strength.

"Man is confronted by many challenges in life," I replied, "by nature, the immensity of the universe, scientific discoveries and the greatest challenge of all is life itself. We must rely on God." I paused to explain myself, "What I am really saying is that Billy's bar mitzvah lessons should continue, just as we had planned."

The father's voice trembled in the silence that followed, and he said, "If the Rabbi is so insistent, let him continue his lessons."

Billy, who sat silently through this exchange with tears in his eyes, mumbled, "If the Rabbi wants me to continue my lessons, I will."

"Of course I would like you to!" I responded.

As I left the house, I prayed fervently for Billy's recovery and that the doctors' prognosis was wrong.

When Billy showed up at our next session, I did not teach him his bar mitzvah *lesson. Instead, I taught him to have faith in God. I knew that he was in distress because he heard that he would die within three months. I shared several stories about faith with him, including some from my experiences against all odds of surviving the Holocaust. Suddenly, he perked up and looked at me.*

"Maybe my stories are reaching him," I thought. We continued to meet, and I encouraged him to believe that God would restore his health, to have trust that healing would come.

Several weeks later, I received an urgent call from Billy's father. My heart felt faint as I answered the call, dreading the news he might have. But his voice was full of elation! "Rabbi!" he said. "I just received a call from doctors in England. A cure has been discovered for the condition that my son has!"

Billy received the new medical treatment and went on to have his bar mitzvah. *He would eventually graduate from high school and attend college, followed by medical school. He became a practicing physician and even went on to win $10 million in the lottery!*

* * *

Billy's story, like Miriam's, illustrates the power of faith in the face of adversity. His faith helped to lift him up, overcome pain, cope with his diagnosis and, most importantly, have hope. Faith is the mother of hope. Hope can lead us out of darkness and despair when doors close around us and lift us up when all seems lost. While Billy's faith wasn't specifically directed at responding to antisemitism or bigotry, it shows the power of perseverance. If we can take this same faith to persevere in our fight against antisemitism, we will maintain hope and never give up.

I tell Billy's story as an example of faith that is not easily found—it must be cultivated. In my work, I am motivated by something Leo Tolstoy once said, "Give me faith, and let me help others to find it." If we can develop our faith, it will sustain us in life and in our efforts to counter adversity, including antisemitism and all forms of hate.

To achieve strong faith is not easy. Hasidic teaching points out that we arrive at faith in two ways: through tradition, such as belief in the God of our forebears, or through inner struggle. For me, faith is a combination of the two—it is validated by tradition, but it is also a product of my own struggle. I have witnessed others achieve faith through the study of religious texts and personal experiences. And I have even seen it develop when people experience the marvels of nature or the majesty of the constellations and stars. Some achieve faith through wandering, and some through a sacred moment. The road to faith might simply be something you feel in your heart. Faith comes from within and from without, and it might even take a lifetime to find your own faith. The more you try, the more you learn and explore, the sooner you will find it. Whichever way faith comes to you, it can uplift your being and inspire you to new heights. It can help you find hope and give you the motivation to work for peace in ways both large and small.

Faith, to me personally, is not only a living reality but also the very essence of life. It is a divine cohesion holding all good together. Acknowledging that some things are beyond our understanding or comprehension is a sign of faith. We bank by faith, we drive by faith, we buy by faith, we marry by faith, we educate our children by faith, we live by faith, and we die by faith. Faith is part of every breath of my life. Without it, we can become negative and lose trust in our neighbors. But through faith, we can revitalize our sense of ethical, moral, and intellectual consciousness that will help us respect our differences and, thereby, respect our neighbors, our community, our country, and the world in which we live.

Faith can also give meaning and purpose to our lives and help us to face fear as it did for Miriam and Billy, and as it has many times for me. We were able to endure misfortunes, including poverty, sickness, and terror, better because of our faith. Where there is such faith, there is less room for fear or anxiety. As the psalmist says, "I fear no evil, for You are with me."[2] When we are confronted with vile antisemitism, our faith can sustain us to continue working toward a more peaceful world.

In addition to my faith in God and my tradition, I have faith in the Jewish People. The core of Jewish vitality and longevity is faith in our very personal God, who is the life force of all humanity and who permeates all. Our ancestors possessed a faith that allowed our People to survive centuries of torture and oppression, and each example is an inspiration and a reason to have hope for the future. For example, for thousands of years, we have had faith that the Divine promise to the patriarchs and the prophets that the land of Israel belonged to their descendants would be realized. This faith carried us through centuries of turmoil and agony. The reconstitution of the State of Israel is, for me, an example of my faith made real.

Prayer helps me to build my faith. I have been a chaplain in the hospital setting for decades and have seen clergy of all religious traditions work together with hospital staff and medical teams caring for patients. These clergy have been actively engaged in the treatment and healing process. Indeed, many medical professionals call upon clergy when patients cease to respond to treatment and all medical means have been exhausted. At such times, prayer and faith remain. Faith through prayer is a dynamic, personal act, flowing between our own hearts and God's love for us. It is reciprocal. Prayer is a meeting point between humans and God. It is an outpouring of one's inner self, a means by which the soul expresses its yearnings and desires. It allows us to verbalize our worries, fears, and frustrations, leading to a sense of relief, helping us to see things in a different way. Prayer is a way of talking things over with God, which can lead to inner peace and help us to generate peace in the world at large.

We all understand that fear, tension, and anxiety have a negative effect on our health that can manifest in physical symptoms. A calm and happy outlook can have the opposite effect. When we have faith, including expressing this through prayer, we draw upon the inexhaustible supply of divine energy. Prayer can empower us to face the difficulties or problems that disturb our emotional and mental equilibrium. In the words of the saintly Rabbi Elimelech of Lizhensk, conceit, anger, envy, jealousy, petty criticism of others, and fault-finding erect a barrier between us and our Creator. Faith and prayer can help to break down this barrier and safeguard our health and peace of mind, giving us the strength to handle what life throws at us.

The Hebrew word for prayer, *lehitpalel*, is a reflexive verb that literally means to "judge oneself." Part of the purpose of prayer is to gain a sense of humility and to engage in self-reflection and self-examination. We cannot allow our egos to become so inflated that our hearts harden. Rabbi Nachman of Breslov, a great Hasidic rabbi, said that humanity must lose itself in prayer and forget its own existence. Rabbi Elimelech of Lizhensk prayed daily for the removal of barriers between our souls and God, asking that we be kept from anger, conceit, evil, and jealousy. He prayed to see the good in fellow human beings. This is a good place to start in fighting hate. When we remind ourselves to find the good in others, we generate less anger and hate and set an example of peacebuilding.

When we pray, we must include the entire world, both the righteous and the evil, our friends and our enemies. Jewish tradition teaches us that we must ask for God's blessings for both our friends and our enemies; we cannot seek God's blessings only for ourselves. I believe that when we pray for those who hate and resent us, we may bring about a change in their attitudes toward us and others. Rabbi Yehuda Halevi, a famous poet and philosopher of eleventh-century Spain, wrote in his *Kuzari* that praying only for oneself is like "refusing to assist fellow citizens in the repair of their walls," while prayer that includes our foes helps us to build peace.[3]

In the synagogue, there is no room for prayers that are merely a recital of one's selfish desires. The Talmud speaks of Jewish solidarity and mutual responsibility and reminds us that: "All the people of Israel are companions; all members of Israel are responsible for one another."[4] This is a reminder that faith is not just a personal journey; we are called to be concerned and care for all God's children. When we bring this into our lives, hate cannot flourish. We can use these ideas to reach across divisions with empathy and compassion and be an example to others.

I have always loved to pray. When I awaken each morning, I thank God for returning me to life, for each day is a new beginning. I pray three times a day and sometimes more. It lifts my spirits, inspires me, and gives me vigor and strength. I have faith in God and in prayer. This is how I feel connected to the Divine being and order. It gives me pleasure and happiness to stand in dignity and strength, acknowledge God's goodness, and pray for all humanity. Rabbi Yehuda Halevi once asked where he might find God, "I sought to come near You, I have called to You with all my heart; and when I went out toward You, I found You coming towards me."[5] I believe prayer brings the Divine closer to our lives.

This way of cultivating faith through prayer helps me to fight hate and antisemitism and to bring more peace into the world. It sustains me, even when I see, as now, that antisemitism is reaching new heights. I know I will never stop fighting for good to prevail, knowing that the fight will be arduous and long. Because of my faith, I still believe that night will be followed by the light of dawn.

Another Miracle That Gave Me Faith

In May 1953, I was nearly twenty-three years old and had survived the Holocaust to find myself living in Brooklyn, New York, with my remaining family, my father

Joseph and my brother Rachmil (now called Robert). I had a few friends and was invited to attend a wedding. I met another young college student at the wedding, Gloria Koslowski. When she learned that I was from Beltiza, she told me the story of a woman she knew who saved a boy from Belitza in a Nazi selection line. Astonished, I said to her, "I am that boy!" I had never forgotten the woman who saved me that day and always hoped that one day I would find her. What a miracle to meet Gloria at this wedding! I learned that Miriam lived in Hartford, Connecticut, and immediately ran to the telephone downstairs and asked the operator to ring Miriam Rabinowitz in Hartford. The operator said, "There are six Miriam Rabinowitzes in Hartford." I said, "Call the first one."

The Miriam I knew answered the phone! I expressed my joy at locating her and my gratitude to her for saving my life. We soon made plans for me to visit her in Hartford, where she had settled with her husband and two daughters. All of them had survived! Another miracle!

My cousin Sam owned a car, so I arranged for him to drive me to visit the Rabinowitz family. When we reached their home in Hartford, she was waiting on the front porch—I had never forgotten her face. I embraced Miriam, got to know her husband Morris, and became reacquainted with their daughters, Ruth and Toby, the two small girls who clung to their mother, along with me, on that fateful day in Zhetl. Both girls were teenagers now, and Ruth was soon to be a college student at the University of Connecticut. Gloria, whom I met at the wedding, was a friend of Ruth's and tragically died in a car accident shortly after I met her. Ruth and I began to write letters to each other, and that summer found ourselves working near each other in the Catskills. A romance bloomed; we were married two years later on December 11, 1955, and we remain married to this day, nearly 70 years later.

* * *

Miriam's faith not only saved my life; it gave me a full life. Neither of us knew, in the split second it took her to make her courageous decision to help me, that we would be connected for life, that we would both survive, that I would marry her daughter and help to raise her three grandsons. All of us lost so much at the hands of the Nazis and their collaborators, but Miriam's act of faith in doing the right thing in the face of vile bigotry has been an inspiration my whole life.

Billy showed me that cultivating faith can lead us through difficult circumstances, sustaining us and giving us resilience. Whenever we experience antisemitism or any kind of bigotry, having faith will help us to keep fighting and never give up. It will also allow us to maintain our hope that things will improve and even that miracles can happen.

I have taken my lessons from Miriam, Billy, my life's experiences, and the Jewish religious tradition to have the faith to stand up for what is right throughout my life. For me, this has meant practicing my faith openly and proudly and sharing it with others, both Jews and non-Jews. It also means praying, which helps me to process all that I have been through, keeps me close to God, and gives me a daily dose of hope. All who have faced violence, trauma, bigotry, and antisemitism need to cultivate hope. My faith has helped me to do that.

Faith has also helped me to advocate for policies and laws designed to reduce hate, such as the Connecticut state mandate to teach about the Holocaust and genocide in our public schools. I have faith that if young people are taught about the past, it is less likely that they will repeat it. My faith also keeps me working closely with leaders of other religious traditions because I believe that when we work together, we generate more brotherly love and interfaith understanding. I have fought against hatred and for peace my whole life, and sometimes it has been very challenging, but my faith never let me give up.

We can all use our faith, no matter how we express it or what our tradition is, to fight intolerance, bias, and violence. Even if you are a person with no particular religious tradition, you can have faith—in yourself, in others, in peace, in the future. You must keep putting one foot in front of the other and know that every small act of kindness and generosity has the potential to dramatically change another person's life. Neither Miriam nor I knew that her action in the few minutes we met in 1942 would ultimately be a crucial step toward my living a long and happy life with a loving wife and family and a career that allowed me the chance to help others along the way. Let my experience be an example of the importance of having faith, doing the right thing, and maintaining hope as tools in the fight against antisemitism and hate.

I know that we live in two worlds—the world that is and the world that we want. Hold on to the world that is and have faith that we can make it into the one we want it to be.

5

Fighting Hate through Friendship

During the Holocaust, when I was living in the woods with my father and brother, we had nothing to shelter ourselves, few items of clothing to keep warm, and little food to eat. We lived in constant fear of discovery. Despite this, there were a small number of Christian farmers we knew in the vicinity of the forest; my father had befriended them long before the war. When they were able, they shared what little food they could with us. These small acts of friendship and kindness helped keep us alive, and I continue to believe in the tremendous power of friendship.

Father John Kiely

The Reverend John Kiely grew up in the Waterbury area of Connecticut. He was ordained as a Catholic priest in Hartford in 1960. After many years at St. Mary's Church in East Hartford and several more at St. Thomas Seminary in the town of Bloomfield, where my congregation was located, Father Kiely moved to the Church of Saint Peter Claver in West Hartford. We first met in the early 1960s when Father Kiely was doing pastoral work at the Institute of Living in Hartford, at the time a prestigious private psychiatric hospital set on acres of beautifully landscaped grounds. The Institute was looking for a Jewish chaplain and I applied for the position. As part of the interview, I gave a sermon to a group of people, including Father Kiely. Afterward, I was asked a few questions. Father Kiely said, "This is the guy." So I was hired.

Our job was to provide religious services to the people receiving treatment at the Institute. I would lead a service on Friday afternoon, and Father Kiely would lead one on Sunday, and we often attended each other's services. Initially, the head of the Institute told me that I could only work with Jewish patients, but Father Kiely stood up and said we should both be able to meet with whoever wanted our help. He stood up for a Jew when it wasn't a common or popular thing to do.

All sorts of people would come to our services. They would also make appointments to see us individually for counseling. Surprisingly, there were several occasions when people asked me about converting to Judaism, and others who asked Father Kiely about converting to Catholicism. I would gently send the Catholics back to Father Kiely, and he would do the same with Jews who came to him seeking conversion.

We found that many people had the same questions for both of us, and since we were both very motivated to help people feel better, we decided to hold a class together. The purpose of the class was to hear questions from the patients and encourage them to talk about what was bothering them. At first, only about eight to ten people showed up, but then word got around. People told others how the class was helping them to talk about their problems, allowing them to hear from others and to feel less alone. Initially, patients would talk only to us, but eventually, they began talking to each other. At that time, this was apparently a new approach, and the class started to increase in size. Eventually, we ran out of space and had to move our class, which grew to more than sixty people, to an auditorium.

The psychiatrists, who in the beginning were not interested in associating with us, began inviting us for lunch in the cafeteria. It was an eye-opener for them to *see how the patients responded to us. We tried to teach people to support each other, to open up to each other by speaking up and joining in friendship, and even sometimes to smile. We taught about humility and faith—in God, humanity, family, friendship, and, importantly, yourself. We also focused on developing friendships and better relationships with family whenever possible.*

I often spoke about the many horrifying things I had been through during the Holocaust and how I had survived and persevered. The patients understood that I knew what suffering felt like, and I stressed the importance of being strong and resilient. I guess I was living proof of the possibility of overcoming the most difficult of circumstances. I never said to them that my way was the only way; instead, I spoke of the inner faith and strength to survive and thrive that I believe they all possessed. I told them that I believed that God created the world for all to live in peace and for all humans to strive to be better. Our shared experience of suffering helped many patients feel comfortable with me.

Father Kiely was also empathetic and connected with his congregants. He had the gift of being able to make friends easily. It was such a blessing for us to meet and have confidence in each other, and we became close, lifelong friends. Our friendship and camaraderie were visible to all we worked with—we hugged each other, ate meals together, and prayed together. We both had cheerful dispositions and were easily able to model a deep and respectful friendship across our differences. Both of us received many letters from patients who told us that, together, we helped them even more than the psychiatrists did!

We respected each other intellectually and enjoyed each other's company. Father Kiely came to our home for dinners and often spoke at the synagogue. Our affection continued to grow over the years. Eventually, Father Kiely told me about another longtime friend of his who worked in the Vatican, a priest who was a secretary to Pope John Paul II. Father Kiely regularly spoke with his friend and told him about my life and our friendship. This friend relayed these stories to the Pope, who was so moved by what he heard that he sent a medal, which Father Kiely presented to me at the fortieth anniversary of our synagogue. I was very honored by this recognition. I framed the medal and accompanying letter, and they hang in my office to this very day.

Unfortunately, Father Kiely developed cancer, and despite the bishop's and his doctor's best efforts, we understood that Father Kiely was going to die. In his will, he directed that I was to deliver his eulogy. At the funeral, when the presiding bishop saw hundreds of priests (evidence of Father Kiely's stature in the church) and only one rabbi, he came to me and asked, "Why do you have the privilege of giving the eulogy?" I told him simply, "He was my friend." I described him to all present as not only a priest but as the wonderful human being he was—a bright and intelligent man of many talents who fulfilled his calling in the most dedicated way. I was grateful to know him and to be his friend.

Eventually, the Institute of Living became part of Hartford Hospital, where I still hold the position of chaplain and continue to visit patients. One day, I was told that the chapel at Hartford Hospital was to be named in my honor. I was indeed very honored, but I asked that Father Kiely's name be placed together with mine, and the hospital agreed. The Lazowski/Kiely Multifaith Chapel at Hartford Hospital is a testament to our great friendship.

* * *

My friendship with Father Kiely is an example of how friendship can be an experience where two people truly connect. Every moment of a friendship, even chatting and laughing together, contains a divine spark. Friendships arise from mutual respect and affection. Choosing a friend is serious business and shouldn't be done haphazardly because friends influence your life.

There are several Hebrew words meaning "friend," and each illustrates a different aspect of friendship. One Hebrew word for friend, "*chaver*," derives from the root meaning "to link oneself" or "to be joined to." Another word, "*rea*," is defined as "one who is close to you, almost like your very self." Another Hebrew term meaning friend is "*yedid*" which is related to two other words, "yad" meaning "hand" and "dod" meaning "loved one." The process of being a friend involves reaching out, extending a hand to another in affection and love. A less frequently used Hebrew word for friend is "*tomech*" meaning "to support."

Each of these Hebrew words highlights a part of friendship. A second-century BCE Hebrew author on ethics, Ben Sira (25:1), states, "My soul takes pleasure in three things, for they are beautiful to the Lord and to all men: harmony among brothers, friendship among neighbors, and a husband and wife suited to each other."

In *Pirkei Avot*, or Ethics of the Fathers (5:16), we are taught about friendship in the following words: "Love that depends on something ceases when the thing it depends on ceases; while love that does not depend on anything will never cease." As an example, the text gives us the story of Amnon and Tamar. Tamar is Amnon's half-sister (both are David's children). Amnon is overcome by passion for Tamar, but his love is based solely on physical desire. Once the incest taboo is violated and Amnon's passion is satisfied, he casts her away, ruining her life. His love was based on one thing, his physical desire, and when that desire was satisfied, he no longer loved her. Love with ulterior motives is destructive.

Conversely, an honest and loving relationship without ulterior motives will never come to an end. An example of such a friendship is that shared between David and Jonathan. The story comes from the book of Samuel (18:3): "And Jonathan sealed a covenant with David's soul and Jonathan loved him like himself." Jonathan made this covenant purely out of love, not to protect himself. He signified this by taking his robe and battle gear, which were most important to him as a warrior, and giving them to David. This covenant was an irrevocable commitment between them. Just as the covenant between God and Israel remains in force even if the people sin grievously, so, too, David and Jonathan committed themselves to each other without reservation. The Torah here bears witness to great friendship as not simply a spiritual bond, but also a covenantal bond, a connection of two souls.

In this chapter of Samuel, King Saul's hatred and Jonathan's love, two opposing emotions, take root. Saul's jealousy of David degenerates into hatred and finally into murderous rage while, in contrast, Saul's son Jonathan comes to love David. This relationship between Jonathan and David has forever become the epitome of loyal friendship. Theirs is a friendship based on love and respect and not on ulterior motives and, thus, endures.

Moses Maimonides explains that friendship based on material self-interest will last only as long as it remains profitable to the parties, but that love based on Godly considerations will endure because spirituality is eternal. Such was the relationship between David and Jonathan, who became fast friends, even though each knew that the other was an obstacle to the throne.

The Talmud also gives advice about friendship when it records the story of a man coming to Rabbi Hillel seeking to be taught "the whole Torah while I stand on one foot." Rabbi Hillel responded, "What is hateful to you, do not do to your friend. That is the whole Torah; the rest is commentary. Go and learn it."[1] This is the concept of friendship that Father Kiely and I shared and showed to the patients at the Institute, to our congregations, and to the wider world.

There is also a Midrash:

A businessman in ancient times from the land of Israel was accused of being a spy. After being condemned to death, the man requests thirty days to return home to put his affairs in order and say goodbye to his family. The judge laughs at the ridiculous request; the man responds that he has a friend who will stay in jail in his place until he comes back—and if he doesn't come back, his friend will die in his place.

This the judge had to see. So, he sent for the convicted man's friend. Sure enough, the man agrees to stand in place of his friend, all the way up to the noose.

The businessman returns home, puts his affairs in order, says goodbye to his family, and returns with time to spare. Unfortunately, there is a storm at sea, and he is delayed. He arrives shortly before the time he is to be executed. He runs to the town square where his friend is already at the gallows; he screams, "No,

it is I who is to be executed!" "And his friend yells back," "No, you're too late!"
They created such a commotion and confusion that the king called for them to be
brought before him.

Each presents his case, and then they begin to argue with each other about
who is to be executed. Finally, the king stops them and says, "I will pardon you
both on one condition—that you make me your third friend!"

* * *

This story shows the power of true friendship, which does not condone wrong
behavior and immoral choices but is there to support, reprove, and help.

Why Friendship?

It is very important to have friends. When people meet, there can be mutual
curiosity; each is interested in knowing something about the other: where they
come from, what their position or profession is, their interests, and so on. Real
friendship is a process-it does not happen overnight. It does not grow in one
hour nor ripen in one day; it grows slowly, gradually while constantly gaining
in depth. It is essential that we have patience with our friends.

It is not good for humans to be alone; we reach our highest levels when we
associate with others. Humans by themselves are lonely, but we experience
profound joy in friendship and love. Without friends, we are isolated; with
friends, we learn from each other, achieve, and grow together. We must be
open-hearted and trust one another. Making sacrifices for friends is also part
of the equation, despite the effort, time, and sometimes drudgery that may be
involved. Look for and be a friend who has a good heart and exhibits mercy,
kindness, and compassion. A close friend can help sustain you, even during
the darkest moments of life.

When we share another's joy, our own pleasure and happiness increase. When we share another's pain, we are saddened as well. A true friend shares feelings, so listen carefully, not only with your ears but also with your heart. To preserve a friendship, three things are necessary: to honor them in their presence, praise them in their absence, and assist them whenever the necessity arises. All the rest are merely ornaments to friendship.

The importance of self-disclosure in friendship was driven home to me when a friend of mine walked into the office wearing a long face. When I asked what was wrong, I got a brush-off, followed by a perfunctory "and are you doing ok?" I was tempted to say sure—no one is comfortable admitting they have problems—but in fact, I did have some things troubling me, and I spilled them out to my friend. Suddenly, our conversation took on a new dimension; not only was my friend supportive of me, but he began to express his own feelings and problems, allowing me to be a friend, to offer encouragement and support to him. As I have learned, when you disclose yourself, you create a climate for others to disclose themselves to you, and the process of friendship is thus deepened and reinforced.

A loving friendship requires friends to listen well to each other and to be tolerant. As the Talmud Yomah (75A) states, "When there is worry in your heart you should tell it to others." However, when you tell your worries to your friends, it is forbidden for them to tell it to others. Your friend's secret is yours alone. Devoted friendship requires loyalty and support. Intolerance is a harsh and unkind attitude toward others, including friends.

The process of friendship requires honesty, and that sometimes means criticism as well. You wouldn't let a friend walk across a crowded room with his fly unzipped or spinach in their teeth. As Rabbi Jose B. Hanina taught, love without criticism is not love. A friend may admonish me for my shortcomings, but his criticism does not aim to humiliate or hurt me. I had a friend whom I always admired for his constructive criticism because it helped me grow. This was because he thoughtfully gave me this advice in private. We must take care not to criticize harshly or embarrass a friend in public. Maimonides warns us to criticize in private, to speak gently and tenderly, and to make clear our interest in the other's welfare. It is neither easy nor comfortable to give or take criticism, but the advice we want to hear is often not the best advice, nor the counsel a true friend should offer us. Being a friend requires us to admit mistakes, to say, "I was wrong" and seek forgiveness. To be a friend, we must be willing to forgive, ready to rectify our errors whenever possible, and forgive ourselves, too.

To be a good friend requires us to be loyal and to stand up for our friends. Rabbi Eliezer taught: "Let the honor of your friend be as dear to you as your own."[2] And Jewish law asserts that if you have something good to say on a friend's behalf, you are forbidden to keep it back.[3] True friendship involves the sharing of the entire range of life's experiences, not only happiness, laughter, celebrations, and success but also disappointment, pain, and tears.

What I have learned is that if you seek perfect friends, you will have no friends at all. A friend is someone who understands your past, believes in your future, and accepts your present—just the way you are. A friend brings out the best in you and expects nothing in return. No one is rich enough to do without a friend. Friends are better than any fortune.

Sheila's Story

In the fall of 1995, my husband and I were expecting our first child and, as a practicing physician, I knew that I would need help at home. A friend recommended that I search for an au pair or nanny and gave me the name of an organization that placed foreign au pairs in American homes. I contacted the organization and filed all the necessary paperwork. In the application, I explained that we were a Jewish family that kept kosher and observed the Jewish holidays. Shortly afterward, I began to receive information on possible matches for our family. One potential match was a fair-skinned, blue-eyed blonde from Düsseldorf, Germany (the information we received included a photo). Alexandra's information contained a statement from her about her family and her experience with young children. I remember that her penmanship was beautiful, and she spoke warmly about the importance of family. So, I scheduled a phone call, the next step in the process. We had a lovely conversation, her English was impeccable, and I explained about keeping a kosher home and our holidays. She was happy and easygoing, and we connected.

Other applicants seemed promising, and I interviewed several of them, but I kept returning to my conversation with Alexandra. She seemed to be the best of the candidates. So why was I hesitating? Well, I come from a family that includes several Holocaust survivors, including one who was in Auschwitz and had prisoner numbers tattooed on his arm. The significance of the Holocaust to my family and to Jews everywhere is part and parcel of who I am, and I was struggling with the idea of inviting a German, whose ancestors may have harmed members of my family or community, into my home to help raise my daughter. I wondered, what does she know about the Holocaust and the Jewish People? I knew that if she was not German, I would have hired her right away. This was causing me sleepless nights.

So, I decided to bring the question to my Rabbi, Philip Lazowski. I had first met him when I was an intern at Mount Sinai Hospital in Hartford, and we had been close ever since. I explained the situation to him, and his response was unequivocal. "You must hire her," he said. "You can't punish her for the possible sins of her grandparents or relatives, you can't assume anything. And, even if they were Nazis you can't punish her for that. If she appears to be like someone you want in your household she should come." Knowing of the Rabbi's experience surviving the horrors of the Holocaust, I admit that I was surprised at how swiftly and the manner in which he answered my question. But I have tremendous respect for Rabbi Lazowski and followed his advice.

I brought her here, and from the moment we met, I knew she was a good match. She came when my first daughter was five weeks old. I trusted her when it was time to go back to work. She was amazing at seventeen years old! She was very respectful of our home rules. Ali was curious about all things Jewish, so I took the opportunity to teach her. She even came to synagogue with us a couple of times. She really learned a lot.

The program only allowed au pairs to stay for one year, but we are still in touch all these years later. She has returned a few times to visit, including for my daughter's bat mitzvah. *Before she visited us, she found a synagogue in Düsseldorf and asked to meet with the Rabbi there to ask questions about the ceremony and to be prepared for this important coming-of-age celebration. Ali never missed our birthdays or Hanukkah.*

She loved our family, and we loved her back. During that first year Ali was here, I told the Rabbi how right he was. When he met Ali, the Rabbi was not surprised that it had worked out. The lesson is that people are good, and we must give them a chance to show us that they are good. I also learned that making friends with those who you think are so different from you can be a powerful experience. I know that because I took a chance so long ago, the Jewish People have one more ally today in Germany, and who knows how many more people will become allies because of her?

* * *

How does friendship help in the fight against antisemitism? It does so in two general ways. First, if you are a member of the Jewish community, having strong friendships with other Jewish People helps in providing a supportive environment, especially in the face of increasing antisemitism. And, second, friendships between Jews and non-Jews help decrease antisemitism.

Jewish community is impossible without friendship. When we trust and love each other, we can build strong communal organizations. When we are loyal and provide constructive criticism in kind ways, we can improve those organizations. Many of us, over the years, have heard a friend say something bigoted or prejudiced, and we need to take to heart the responsibility to gently inform and educate our friends when they do such things. This helps them to become better people and to avoid further embarrassment. When we develop strong friendships, we support each other in life's celebrations, such as weddings, births, *b'nai mitzvot*, graduations, and Jewish holidays. We can also be there in difficult times. When we share Shabbat and holidays with our friends, we not only deepen our connection to each other, but we also connect to the Jewish People and our faith. When our community is targeted with Zoom bombings (when antisemites invade virtual events), vandalism, harassment, bomb threats, or worse, we will also be there to support each other and demand action from the authorities. Building a strong community starts with friendships.

My friendship with Father Kiely was special to me in so many ways. We enjoyed each other's company for decades, both professionally and socially. Our friendship across our different faiths allowed us to do good work that affected untold numbers of people who were suffering. Because of our friendship, we were able to learn about each other's faiths and practices. While, of course, we had many differences, we also realized that we had much in common. We were then able to take what we learned from each other and spread that information to our respective communities. Supporting and expanding this mutual understanding helps to reduce hate, including antisemitism. Whenever either of us had questions for the other, we felt comfortable asking them. This deep understanding allowed us to share our warm relationship beyond just the two of us. Publicly honoring me with a medal from the Pope declared Father Kiely's value of our relationship for all to see, and asking me to speak at his funeral showed the many people in attendance how important friendship and understanding across faiths can be. I did the same by including his name on the chapel at the hospital. Sheila's story tells us the importance of not judging other people because of their heritage or background, or simply because they are different from ourselves. What opportunity would have been missed if Sheila had not overcome her fear? Like Sheila, we can all reach across divides and create lasting friendships and, in doing so, build bridges of understanding.

Over the years, I have made it a priority in my life to cultivate friendships with those of other faiths. In Bloomfield, we had monthly meetings of all the clergy to discuss local issues of importance, and through this, I became friends with many of them. Reverend Alvan Johnson of the American Methodist Episcopal Church in Bloomfield is a good friend. I have invited him to speak to my congregation, and he has done the same for me. Archbishop Leroy Bailey of the First Cathedral, the largest Black church in Connecticut, has been a friend of mine for over forty years and when I was asked to come to the dedication of his very first church, I gave a blessing and prayed that he would be successful and that the church would grow under his leadership. My prayers were answered, and we remain great friends to this day.

Every one of you reading this can make friends and, in doing so, reduce the amount of hate in the world. You can treat your friends with love and care, be a good listener, and be a gentle voice of criticism when required. Learn from them and try to understand the challenges they face in life, and do what you can to be a support to them. And when someone different from you, in whatever way that may be, asks to share something of their faith, ethnicity, or background with you, take it as a chance to understand them better. A local organization that Rev. Johnson is very active in and that supports interfaith understanding uses the motto: When we understand each other more, we hurt each other less. What better way to do this than by making friends?

6

Standing Up Together with Courage

Having survived the Holocaust, I understand how important it is to stand up to hate and antisemitism. When hate reaches its most deadly—when a marginalized people are killed by the millions in a years-long government-sponsored genocide—it becomes very difficult to stand against it. This is why it is so important to push back against antisemitism and hate long before it reaches this level. We must always be armed with pride in ourselves and our tradition, as well as collaboration, education, and advocacy skills to stand up to hateful words and actions before they turn violent. One of my former congregants tells the following story of standing against antisemitism and, in the process, being an advocate for all victims of bias and bigotry.

Susan's Story

Civil rights laws in place for decades have made it illegal to discriminate on the basis of race, sex, religion, disability, or national origin. But does this apply to the jury room? This is my story.

More than a decade ago, a former employee threatened to sue our family business, alleging that she was wrongly terminated. As any small business owner will tell you, when someone threatens a lawsuit, the worst thing that can happen is for it to land in court, no matter its merit (it takes time and money). In this case, the judge urged the plaintiff to settle with us for what the judge viewed as a quite generous settlement amount. However, the plaintiff demanded much more and the case landed in a St. Louis courtroom to be heard by a jury.

After several weeks, the jury found in favor of the plaintiff, awarding her compensatory and punitive damages that amounted to about double the pretrial settlement offer (about $140,000).

Within moments of the jury's dismissal, a member of the jury made a beeline for our attorney. She introduced herself as a retired Catholic librarian. She went on to say that she had experienced the most vile, repulsive antisemitic comments during the jury's deliberations, calling my husband a "rich Jew doc" and me "a rich Jew bitch" and "a penny-pinching Jew." A second Catholic juror also complained about the antisemitic "flavor" of the deliberations.

Our jury of "peers" had included no Jews at all; had these "righteous gentiles" not come forward, no one would have known about the bigotry that took place in the jury room.

The judge, after reviewing these two jurors' statements and interviewing the entire jury, concluded that the antisemitic incidents had likely taken place. In spite of this, he ruled that he did not have the authority to set aside the jury's decision and order a new trial, and he directed us to the Appellate Court for further relief.

An appeal would entail more time, money, and distress, with the best outcome being a new trial. Any rational person would pay the verdict and walk away, right?

We sought advice from friends, local rabbis, and Jewish leaders. Without exception, they all recommended that the decision should be based solely on business considerations and that nothing more would be gained by appealing the jury's verdict. Some even argued that there wasn't that much antisemitism in the St. Louis area and that the deliberations were a "one in a million" event.

Only one voice in my local community softly spoke up in favor of pursuing an appeal: an elderly woman and Holocaust survivor who wondered aloud whether the Shoah *would have happened "if more people had spoken out when they still could."*

Surprised and disappointed by this near unanimity in advice that conflicted with my deepest instincts, I called my childhood rabbi to seek his counsel in the matter. As a survivor himself, Rabbi Lazowski has been outspoken in his fight against genocide, whether it be against Jews, Rwandans, or other marginalized peoples. Without the slightest hesitation, he forcefully expressed the need for each and every Jew to fight antisemitism wherever it rears its ugly head. He offered moral and rabbinical support as well as various avenues for funding if the need arose. In his celebrated no-nonsense style, Rabbi Lazowski said that "the two Catholic jurors had more brains than your local rabbi!"

Based largely on this conversation, we appealed the verdict on multiple grounds, including the claim of juror misconduct. While the Appellate Court did order a new trial, it did so based on grounds other than jury misconduct. It considered the offensive behavior to be "extremely rare" and unworthy of further comment. But this wasn't the end—the plaintiff appealed to the state Supreme Court.

A panel of seven Missouri Supreme Court judges ruled unanimously that,

When a juror makes statements evincing ethnic or religious bias or prejudice during deliberations . . . the juror has revealed that he is not fair and impartial. Whether the statements may have had a prejudicial effect on other jurors is not necessary to determine. Such statements evincing ethnic or religious bias or prejudice deny the parties their constitutional rights to a trial by 12 fair and impartial jurors and equal protection of the law.

In other words, a victory!

What have I learned from this, besides that the search for justice is a long, expensive, and emotional process? I have learned that we must pursue justice, no matter how small a contribution we think we will make, and that we must celebrate those, like the jurors who came to us with this information, who stand up for what's right, even when there is a personal cost. And, more importantly, we must stand up for ourselves and the Jewish community and squelch the very first stirrings of antisemitism, even if they are only words uttered in the privacy of a jury room.[1]

* * *

Susan and her husband showed tremendous courage in the face of antisemitism and stood up even when few in their community would take it seriously. Their courage and perseverance resulted in a ruling by the highest court in their state that bigotry and prejudice have no place in the jury room. This is not only a judgment that refuses to accept antisemitism, but it also protects the constitutional rights of other, non-Jewish, litigants. To me, this is a great example of the benefits of standing up for what is right and fighting against hate; the benefits expand beyond your circle and into the wider world.

The Torah states that when the Israelites (*b'nei yisrael* or the children of Israel) sought their freedom from Egyptian enslavement, they went up out of *Mitzrayim*, the land of Egypt, "*chamushim*" or armed.[2] Rashi, the great eleventh-century commentator, interprets "*chamushim*" to mean "*mizuyanim*" or armed with weapons. Similarly, earlier in the Torah, when Abram (later named Abraham) seeks to rescue captive kinsmen with an armed group, Onkelos, the great first-century BCE commentator, renders *chamushim* as "*mezerzin*," saying that Abram armed his men with weapons.[3]

At first glance, it is puzzling that *b'nei yisrael* needed weapons. After all, when the fleeing Israelites reached the *yam-suf* (the Sea of Reeds in English, also incorrectly but commonly translated as the Red Sea), they did not lift a finger against the army of Egyptians who were pursuing them as they escaped;

no weapons were needed for them to be free. Rather, in that instance, Moses assured them *"Hashem lachem v'atem tacharishun,"* God will do your battle for you and you will be silent.[4]

If so, why did the Israelites need to be armed with weapons? It may be that they would need these weapons later when encountering unfriendly tribes on their way to the Promised Land. In Josh. 1:14, as *b'nei yisrael* are about to enter the land of Israel, Rashi returns here to his point that *chamushim* again means armed. This biblical narrative has a wonderful lesson for us to learn—when the Jewish People are fighting for their place in the world, their freedom, and their right to exist and to defend themselves, they must be armed. This is an obligation. But what are our armaments in the fight against antisemitism and hate?

My former congregant, Susan, and her husband showed us one of the tools at our disposal in fighting antisemitism—standing up and fighting it wherever it arises. They refused to back down in the face of blatant, ugly antisemitic words and attitudes. At the same time, the two jurors who came forward were also examples of people who dared to do the right thing and report the bias and bigotry they witnessed. They could easily have said nothing and returned to their lives. They could not have anticipated that their reports of antisemitism would one day result in a change in the law that would support greater dignity for all who come before juries in Missouri. The tools of standing up, speaking out, and showing courage are weapons in the fight against hate that are available to all of us. Perhaps when we use these "weapons" effectively, we can avoid having to use weapons of war later.

Sometimes, however, much more is required of us. During the Second World War, all the Jews in my hometown were rounded up; placed in ghettos; had all their homes, businesses, and belongings stolen; and most were eventually murdered by the Nazis and their local collaborators. My mother, my sister Rachel, and my brothers, Aaron and Abraham were among those brutally murdered. Being armed in this situation called for more from us to be able to survive. Many times in those years, I yearned for an actual gun to fight the Nazis.

By the grace of God, I survived the selections and massacres and reunited with my brother Rachmil. We later learned that my father, uncle, and aunt were still alive. We were able, despite the immense danger and daily threat of death, to journey into the forest and locate the small group that they were hiding with. It was a miracle on top of more miracles that we had survived this long and were able to find each other.

* * *

Life in the forest was a daily, even hourly, test of our ability and will to survive. We had only the clothes on our backs, no shelter, no medical supplies, few tools, and only the food we could forage, beg from friendly farmers, or steal. When it rained, we were soaked to the bone; when it was cold, we huddled together for warmth. The insects, lice, fleas, mosquitoes, and more were relentless, and some transmitted typhus. Many people died from these difficult conditions.

Our faith in God, our tradition, and in each other sustained us, and while we lived in fear and suffering every minute of every day, we also witnessed miracles. Our faith and will to survive were our acts of resistance.

While we were in the woods, a child had been born to a woman from Belitza, a baby boy with strong lungs. One day, when he was about four months old, we were out of our hiding place when we heard the sounds of gunfire. We could tell that German soldiers were but a few hundred feet away and heading in our direction. Everyone quickly took cover. I ran into nearby shrubs, pressing my body into the earth, praying that we would not be discovered.

Then it happened. The baby began to wail. I could see other adults motioning to the mother to silence the child, which, of course, she had been trying to do all along. Everyone was panicking.

In desperation, the mother covered the mouth of the baby with her hand and pressed firmly to stifle the cries. Shortly, the sound ceased. A sort of calm stillness settled over the child. He was motionless and appeared to turn a bit blue.

Still, the Germans approached.

The devastated mother left the child for dead, and we all ran to another location that provided better cover. We waited and waited; eventually, the gunfire stopped, and the forest was quiet. The Nazis had left.

This young mother had made a terrible sacrifice to save our group. We surely would have been found had the baby not been silenced, and we were heartbroken. This infant had represented a small victory against the murderous Nazi regime— new Jewish life. To see it snuffed out was a new depth of sorrow.

That night, our group discussed what had transpired, and it was decided that my father and another member of the group would try to find the ill-fated baby and provide a proper burial for him. When they arrived at the spot where the baby had been left, they were astonished. There before them was a happy, healthy baby, gurgling away and kicking his lively feet in the air. He had survived the ordeal!

My father picked up the baby and quickly brought him to his distraught mother. She, who had been half-crazed with grief, clutched the healthy baby, squeezed him to her breast, and cried tears of joy.

From then on, this baby became a symbol of our resistance and survival. We all took responsibility for his care and did everything we could to prevent harm to him. It's possible that, without all this doting and attention, he never would have survived our time in the woods. In providing for him and ensuring his survival, we committed to our survival and a future for Jews. He helped us to reclaim our humanity and, for some, their faith. He gave us hope.

* * *

This young mother's act of sacrifice in stifling her baby's cries was an incredibly courageous decision made with little time to think. Her actions saved *all* of us. I was still a child myself, and even I recognized the impossible choice that this young woman faced. It was only years later, when I was blessed with three sons of my own, that the true weight of what she had done became even more significant to me. Her actions remind me of the story of the binding of Isaac. In the Torah, Abraham is told by God to take his son, Isaac, to the top of a mountain and build an altar upon which to sacrifice him. At the last minute, God spares Isaac and provides a ram for the sacrifice. The circumstances of the Holocaust called upon this young mother to make a similar sacrifice, to save the lives of many more, and her faith and courage led to her action. And, like the story of Isaac, her son, too, was spared. There is a Yiddish expression that translates as "money lost, nothing lost; courage lost, everything lost." This young mother proved the opposite: courage found, everything found.

It is my fervent hope that no one is called upon to make such choices in their lives, and at the same time, we can all recognize that sometimes the courage we need to take action to fight hate and bigotry may require extra work and even sacrifice on our part. And when we fight antisemitism, hate, and prejudice, there is a good chance that we are saving others, even people we may not know, in the process. May the reward for such courage be just as great.

The other lesson I take from this story is that once the baby was found alive, we all pitched in to care for him. There is strength in standing up against hatred together. Sometimes the fight is very hard, and to have someone standing by your side keeps you going. One of the mottos I live by is "never give up," and this is easier when we have partners in the work of fighting hate. The survival and care for this infant were also an example of our uniting to invest in the future. While we were fighting every minute just to survive to the next, we were investing our little extra energy in ensuring that this small Jewish child would live to see a future without Nazis, and where he could grow up, have a *bar mitzvah*, marry, and create his own family. Our care for him gave us hope for a Jewish future. Working in unity toward a safe and secure future is a way each of us can stand up to hate every day. We are all stronger when we are armed with the chance to live freely and openly.

* * *

We also had help in the forest. First, there were a few friendly farmers and people from local towns who risked their lives to provide us with occasional potatoes, bread, apples, or other small bits of food that they could spare. Some of these were people whom members of our group knew from before the war, and these relationships and courageous acts of generosity helped to save us.

And there were Partisan fighters in the forest as well. Many of these groups were fighters from the Soviet Army, some working with escaped Jewish fighters who had joined them. Sometimes these Jewish fighters were open about their identities; other times they felt it was safer to hide that they were Jews. There were also groups led and populated by Jewish survivors. There were thousands of these Jewish Partisan fighters in the woods of Eastern Europe. They were another way that we stood up and fought back.

In the more than two years that I spent hiding from the Nazis in the woods, I was fascinated by the Partisans and yearned to meet them and to fight with them. I was only thirteen, and they would not take recruits younger than fifteen. In addition, my father had already lost his wife and three of his children, and I was not sure that, had I been old enough, he would have let me risk my life in this new way. Even so, I dreamed of joining them and knew that I would never allow myself to be captured or killed by the Germans, and, as they did, I would save a bullet for myself.

In the fall of 1943, about fifteen Partisans rode on horseback into our camp. I was thrilled to meet them and hear their stories. We learned that the Partisans, including Jewish resistance fighters, were engaged in armed combat with the German military and that they were also very involved in acts of sabotage that disrupted supply lines to the German forces. Sometimes they were able to divert these supplies to the Partisans and even to some of the family groups hiding in the forest. We knew that these efforts were making it harder for the Germans to succeed at the front with the Soviet Union and enjoyed the moments when we could hear of the successes of these resistance fighters.

At one point, some Partisans had captured a young Nazi soldier alive, and they led him past our family group on their way to bring him to their commander. He was a Nazi without a gun, unarmed. He begged for his life. Without any of us saying anything or asking any questions, he blurted out in German, "I did not kill Jews." Whether or not this was true, the treatment of Jews appeared to weigh on his conscience. I admit, if I had had a gun at that moment, I would have killed him. Alone, without a gun, he was pathetic; he was like nothing to me. I never learned what happened to him.

I was never able to join these fighters as our area was liberated shortly before I turned fifteen. But I admired and respected their ability to fight against the Nazi machine and to use their courage and intellect to contribute to the eventual victory of the Allied forces. They brought hope to our small group trying to eke out an existence and stay alive while hiding from the Nazis. And hope was an important element in our ability to withstand hardship. I will be forever grateful to the Partisans, Jewish and non-Jewish alike.

* * *

The Partisans and the resistance fighters were another example of standing up to hate under the most extreme circumstances. After the war, I went to school and became a rabbi. Since then, my life has been about working for peace in every way possible. I do not advocate violence. However, I respected the work of these fighters, including and especially the Jewish ones, whose livelihoods and families had been taken from them. While they sometimes had to kill enemy combatants, they most often had to work strategically and tactically to interrupt the progress of the war. The Partisans so terrorized the German Wehrmacht that they were afraid to enter the woods. The Partisans eventually did so much damage in our area that no train could deliver food, ammunition, or warm clothes to the front; every bridge was burned.

Like these fighters, we must work together, Jews and non-Jews, to be successful in combating bigotry. As Rabbi Jonathan Sacks famously said, "The hate that starts with the Jews never ends with the Jews." It is in the interest of all of us to work together to fight antisemitism and all forms of hate, and like the Partisans, we are more effective when we work together. The seven nations with the largest populations of Jews today (the United States, Canada, the United Kingdom, Germany, France, Argentina, and Australia), known as the J7, are working together to fight antisemitism.[5] They regularly meet to understand issues, communicate, and coordinate their responses to antisemitism. The J7 can be a lesson and inspiration for all of us.

And, like the Partisans and Jewish resistance fighters, we too must act strategically and tactically in disrupting hate and antisemitism. This can sometimes mean picking the right cases to file lawsuits about, focusing on the right legislators, working with the right partners to pass legislation, and speaking up for ourselves and others who are the targets of bias.

We can also be inspired by the Holocaust survivors who came to America, broken and penniless, after enduring the unthinkable and who did not back down. They had the courage to rebuild their lives from nothing. We can emulate their faith, pride in their heritage, and belief in each other. Like them, we must not back down or be intimidated. If we have the courage of our convictions, respect for each other, and love for our community and our homeland, our enemies will not succeed. We must be bold and creative and radiate a light that illuminates the world with love, hope, and lasting peace.

All my life, I have stood for peace and against prejudice and hate. I endured history's darkest hour as a child in the Holocaust and witnessed how easy it is for people to move from words and attitudes to restricting rights, then to crimes against property, and eventually to crimes against humanity. The world again saw a rapid descent into mass violence in Rwanda in 1994, where the verbal dehumanization of one group swiftly morphed into mass murder.

We can arm ourselves with strategic and tactical weapons by using our intelligence, education, and advocacy efforts. We can also be armed with knowing our own history, understanding the multitude of ways that antisemitism can present itself, and vocally calling it out. We need to educate others about antisemitism as well; this is another weapon in our arsenal. Working together with other Jews and the Jewish community at large shows that we are unified in our fight against antisemitism and gives courage to each of us to continue this effort. And, of course, partnering with others outside the Jewish community amplifies the message that antisemitism is unacceptable everywhere.

The Nazi who was captured by the Partisans had no weapons, literal or figurative, that could save him. When I was struggling to stay alive in the forest during the Holocaust, I did not think that I had any "weapons" available to me either. But I now see that our love and care for each other, along with our resilience, ingenuity, and adaptability, meant we actually were "*chumasim*" or armed. Remember the baby who miraculously lived and for whom we all took responsibility? Well, he lived a full and productive life and remains alive today; he even has great-grandchildren.

7

The Importance of Education

Education can be used to divide people and teach hate. In America, we have a history of enslaving Black people and denying them any education. Then under Jim Crow, the education system segregated Black and white Americans. Our country employed schools that denied Native Americans the ability to retain their languages, beliefs, and cultures. The education system in Poland and Germany before the Second World War discriminated against Jews and prevented them from accessing education.

But we also know that education that helps students understand, respect, and accept people who are different from them is critical in the fight against hate. Teaching about the Holocaust and other genocides, including those in Cambodia, Burma/Myanmar, Rwanda, and more, is a way to show students how biased and bigoted words and attitudes can evolve into violence and eventually genocide. And it can help students remember to address hate in the early stages before it's too late.

* * *

For decades, I would visit middle and high school classrooms and assemblies all over the state to talk about my experience of surviving the Holocaust. I would, of course, tell of the horrors that I witnessed and the fear that I lived with. And I would also speak of the miracles that saved me, the love of my family, and the sustenance I took from my faith. I also encouraged the students to work hard in school and continue to learn, including about the events that led up to the Holocaust and other genocides, such as those in Cambodia and Rwanda. I always emphasized the importance of education. I told them that education was a strong value in my family, and continuing to learn was one way to honor the members of my family who were murdered by the Nazis.

Not that long ago, I was speaking at a prestigious private boarding school. After my talk, a young Black man came up to me. I thought he might have a question or simply want to thank me for telling my story. He told me, however, that he had heard me speak when he was in middle school. He said that he was profoundly affected by my story and took my words to heart. He wrote this about his experience:

> I got goosebumps as soon as I listened to Rabbi speak about his experience. . . . This was my second time hearing him, and my 8th Holocaust survivor I have been blessed to meet. . . . The first time I heard him speak upon his experience was in 8th grade . . . after we had just finished reading "Night" by Elie Wiesel. I cried my first time listening to him as a 12-year-old, I immediately felt an impact from Rabbi. His speech on faith has motivated me on and off the baseball field, school, and in life through tough times that we all face. Faith is what we must hold within us even at our highest points in life because we never know when we will need it. God chose Rabbi to live through those times and make it to today so that we can all receive the message to not repeat history and to realize that we are all one and shall not harm each other over the smallest conflicts. Rabbi also spoke upon being educated, we shall educate ourselves as much as possible because with education no evil shall ignite against humanity.[1]

I was pleased that my story was a source of inspiration for this young man and wished him all the best. I know that he will also take my story with him, be alert to, and stand up against prejudice when he encounters it.

* * *

One of the reasons I like talking to students and young people, in general, is that many of them have never heard from a survivor of genocide, and sharing my story allows them to experience what it feels like to be a Jew and to have survived the Holocaust. Studying the Holocaust helps students to understand the roots of prejudice and stereotyping in any society, not just in Europe in the middle of the past century. It also allows students to see the dangers of remaining silent, apathetic, and indifferent in the face of bias and bigotry, including antisemitism.

Over the years, I have received countless letters from the young people I have spoken with. Often, they simply thank me for teaching them and for being willing to reopen deep wounds in doing so. One letter said, "*You really taught me that it is better to share one's past in order to prevent history from repeating itself.*" While another student wrote, "*Every Holocaust survivor should tell his or her story.*" Many students appreciated hearing from me in-person and articulated that this impacted them in ways that reading textbooks had not, with one writing, "*I loved being able to learn from a first-person account and I will remember this for a long time.*" Hearing my story affected students in ways the classroom had not. One teacher wrote to me saying, "*I have sat through 14 years' worth of assemblies and never have I seen an audience as captivated. . . . You do honor to the victims and impart wisdom about how to live.*" Students also mentioned the impact of hearing from a witness to the events of the Holocaust, as one put it, "*I had never seen all the kids so entranced, even the middle schoolers who normally can't sit still were in awe of your story.*" And more recently, a student wrote, "*I've never seen so many students NOT on their phones!*"

The students are also very empathetic, and many of them express relief and gratitude that I survived and found my future wife after such difficult times. As one student put it, "*Your story was one of great hope and love.*" It is important to me that people leave my talks with a sense of hope. As I have said before, my faith gives me hope and the strength to carry on. Many students see the importance of faith in my story. One wrote to me, "*You have taught me what it truly means to remain unwavering in your faith and how to fight against all odds, even in the face of overwhelming adversity.*" Others recognized that my faith helped me to persevere, noting that I "*never gave up*" and that my story helped them to "*believe that I can overcome anything as long as I have faith.*" Students also understood that "*a lot of people lost faith because of the Holocaust and to see someone like you really gives people hope*" and that hearing about my faith "*was a wonderful inspiration, as well as a great example for me to follow.*" Of course, most of these students were not Jewish, so I am grateful that they understand that, even though their faith may be expressed differently from mine, it is an important quality to cultivate in the fight against hate and hardship.

When teaching students, the first question I ask is, "Do you know the word Holocaust?" Most of the students have little to no knowledge of the topic. I realized that many of the students had never heard the word Holocaust, had never studied this period of history, and were not discussing it at home. Statistics show that my experience in Connecticut was not unusual; many Americans have never read about and know very little about the Holocaust and the events that led up to it. Students I have taught have written to me about how much they learned from hearing my story. One letter writer said, "*I didn't know a lot about the Holocaust and how it affected people's lives before you came. But after you came and talked to us I learned so much,*" while another wrote, "*I am now more knowledgeable about the Holocaust and you helped to cement the symbolism and importance of that event in my mind.*" Learning about the Holocaust helped many young people to appreciate the lives they have in America, as one wrote, "*Your story helped me realize how lucky I am,*" and another acknowledged their naivete and said, "*You opened my eyes to what is good in the world.*" I heard from one student who wrote, "*You made me realize how good we have it now . . . the story you told will be instilled in my mind forever.*" One teacher noted, "*Your efforts have a tremendous impact on our students in helping them appreciate the advantages they have today. Hopefully the world will become better because of the lessons our students have learned from you."* I see this as another important aspect of Holocaust education—appreciating the democratic system we live in, and I hope that this appreciation means that students will be inspired to protect it.

Just as important, many students, after learning about the Holocaust, vowed to remember what happened and incorporate the lessons into their lives. As I have said before, we have to know what happened in the past so that we do not repeat it, and many of these students took that idea to heart. One wrote, *"I will not forget the wise words you expressed and will never forget the lessons I've learned from you."* Another told me, *"I will remember your words for the rest of my life as I struggle through some of the minor hardships I will have to endure. I can only thank you from the bottom of my heart as your words will continue to shape my life for the better."* Others combined their vow to remember with a commitment to take action: *"The best that I can do is always remember the events that happened to you and pass them on to my children. And also to do everything in my power to make sure that an event to the scale of the Holocaust does not occur in the future."* Some were *"motivated to tell others of your stories and books so they can learn and be just as inspired as I am."* Still, others recognized the importance of standing up to hate and said they would incorporate this lesson into their lives: *"I will take your advice on standing up for what's right and how to make change. It's important to know the truth about history, and your stories helped me understand that,"* and *"I was motivated by your call to action about not standing by while something bad is happening."* Hearing from so many students affected by my teaching confirmed for me how Holocaust education, especially concerning where hateful words and ideas can lead, is critically important to addressing antisemitism and all forms of hate. A scholar has noted that the Holocaust is "unprecedented [because it was central to Nazi ideology] . . . but it is not unique. If it were unique, we could forget about it, because it could happen only once. But it could happen again . . . we want to avoid that."[2] I believe that this kind of learning must happen continuously and in every generation.

Telling my story in other venues, outside the classroom, also reached young people.

* * *

Many years ago, I was interviewed about a return visit I had recently made to my hometown. During a road-building project, a mass grave with thirty-six Jewish victims of the Nazi regime had been discovered there. The victims included my beloved Rabbi, Shabtai Fein. I remember how the Nazis had tortured and humiliated him. They strapped him, like a beast of burden, to a cart and made him pull it. They forced him to wash horses and then drink the dirty water, and when he could drink no more, they forced more on him until he died. Even once he was dead, they continued to beat him. It was pure evil, and I was to witness similar sadistic behavior time and again through the course of the Holocaust.

As I was the only survivor from our town who was also a rabbi, I was asked to lead a memorial service for the remains of these unfortunate souls. The story about my experience was published in two articles in a local newspaper.

One morning shortly after this, there was a knock at my door. I opened the door, and standing before me was a small boy of about nine or ten years old, completely alone, bearing a large basket of fruit. He said, "I read your story in the newspaper and I wanted to bring you a present and meet you." I was speechless. I learned that this child was from a Christian family that lived on a farm in Glastonbury, a town several miles away, and that he had navigated several buses and a long walk to arrive at my house. He must have left very early in the morning.

I told him that I admired and appreciated his gesture and asked what I could do for him. He said, "I would like you to give me a blessing." I happily complied with his wish. After a short visit, he went on his way.

Years later, I was speaking at an event at a local university, and after the event, a woman and a young man came up to speak to me. This was the boy who had brought me the fruit basket, all grown up, along with his mother. She had come to thank me. She told me that this son had become prosperous in ways that her other children had not, and she believed it was because I had blessed him when he visited me so many years ago. I told her that I was sure it was due to this young man's perseverance and hard work and not my blessing. She disagreed with me and continues to attend events where I have been invited to speak.

* * *

My experience in telling my story and the response I received from students, teachers, and others over the years inspired me to advocate for a statewide law mandating the study of the Holocaust and other genocides in our schools. I saw the passing away of so many of the older survivors and knew that there would come a day when students would no longer be able to hear firsthand testimony from those who lived through the Holocaust. I learned that New Jersey was the first state to pass a Holocaust education mandate in 1994, and some others had followed suit in the intervening years. I felt it was time for Connecticut to do the same.

I was a chaplain for the State Senate, so I began reaching out to legislators. I was invited to speak to the education committee, where I presented my case on how important I believed it was to learn about the Holocaust and other genocides that have happened since, including in Africa and Asia. But it felt like the legislation was going nowhere. Eventually, I gave my book, *Faith and Destiny*, about my experience in the Holocaust, to a state senator from New Haven. She told me she started reading it and finished it in one night because she was so engrossed in the story. And, with tears in her eyes, she thanked me. I asked her to introduce legislation requiring the teaching of the Holocaust and genocide in public schools. She agreed and helped shepherd the bill through its passage. It took several years, but the bill finally passed by unanimous votes in both chambers of the state legislature and was signed into law on May 10, 2018, making Connecticut the tenth state to require teaching about genocide and the Holocaust. At the signing, Lieutenant Governor Nancy Wyman said,

> Young people must understand the devastating and permanent consequences of the Holocaust. With soaring oratory and singular legislative actions that codified supremacy, the Nazis built an extermination machine that virtually wiped out East European Jewry. Students must be taught this history, not just to ensure their vigilance in preventing future genocide, but also so they recognize the opportunities they have every day to speak out against hate and injustice and recognize how racism happens. These small acts of good shape a future of equality—and they start with education.[3]

About half of all states now require similar education. Now is the time for all of us to come together to learn the best ways to teach this subject and ensure that it continues long after the last survivor is gone.

Inspired by this concern, my son, Alan, joined me and other survivors, along with their children and grandchildren, in the founding of a nonprofit organization dedicated to educating our community about the Holocaust. It is called Voices of Hope.[4] We believe that the children and grandchildren of Holocaust survivors can promote the memory of those who perished during the Holocaust and honor those still alive. We must come together to tell their stories and educate the world so that future generations know what happened and can work to prevent future violence based on hatred. Voices of Hope provides education, books and curricula, commemorative events, field trips, speakers, scholarships, training, and resources for educators in Connecticut. Events include community-wide commemorations for Yom HaShoah and International Holocaust Remembrance Day, as well as public education events like the Descendants of the Shoah Conference and public awareness programming. Voices of Hope knows that firsthand accounts by survivors provide compelling testimony, as I have witnessed. But as fewer survivors remain to tell their stories, Voices of Hope has taken on the task of training and educating descendants of Holocaust survivors to continue to retell their families' stories.

There are similar organizations in other states, as well as national organizations like the United States Holocaust Memorial Museum,[5] Echoes and Reflections,[6] and the USC Shoah Foundation,[7] working to make sure that people have access to quality information about the Holocaust and other genocides. A 2020 study illustrated the benefits that I have seen in Holocaust education and found that:

- Eight out of ten college students report having received at least some Holocaust education during high school. The majority received one month or less of Holocaust education. More than 55 percent reported watching either in-person or video survivor testimony.

- Students with Holocaust education reported greater knowledge about the Holocaust than their peers who did not receive Holocaust education; 78 percent of students with Holocaust education reported "knowing a lot or a moderate amount about the Holocaust," compared to 58 percent of students with no Holocaust education.

- Students with Holocaust education have more pluralistic attitudes and are more open to differing viewpoints, which includes being more comfortable with people of a different race or sexual orientation. They are also significantly more likely to report a willingness to challenge incorrect or biased information (28 percent more likely), challenge intolerant behavior in others (12 percent more likely), and stand up to negative stereotyping (20 percent more likely).

- When presented with a bullying scenario, students with Holocaust education reported being more likely to offer help and were 50 percent less likely to do nothing.

- Students exposed to Holocaust education demonstrate higher critical thinking skills and a greater sense of social responsibility and civic efficacy if survivor testimony is part of their experience.[8]

More recent research has revealed additional benefits. Studies show that people who knew that 6 million Jews were killed in the Holocaust "believed the fewest anti-Jewish tropes" and those who had Holocaust education in schools endorsed fewer antisemitic beliefs.[9] This shows that high school education on the Holocaust is correlated with reduced antisemitism, increased openness to differing viewpoints, and helps to build civic efficacy. The data on providing this education in schools "is consistent with past findings that showed those who get their information about the world from mainstream news outlets had lower rates of belief in anti-Jewish ideas than those who received their information from the internet or other sources."[10] By providing this education in schools, educators can address the prevalence of mis/disinformation and teach students how to critically evaluate sources. This ability is essential given the rise of false information about the Holocaust and other historical events. Furthermore, those who received Holocaust education showed "higher rates of critical thinking and a greater willingness to challenge intolerant behavior."[11]

It has also been found that by showing that the underlying sources of hate and antisemitism that drove the Holocaust still exist today, "students can gain a deeper understanding of the impact of hate and the importance of combating it" and build "a fluid historical arc . . . to grapple with the long history of antisemitism as conspiratorial thinking."[12] This report concludes that "these findings strongly support the need for more and higher quality education on the Holocaust."

Imagine the impact if all fifty states and all territories of the United States required high-quality Holocaust and genocide education. I know that the way the Holocaust is studied across the country is variable. Some places only do this work for an afternoon, while others offer semester-long courses with field trips to former concentration camps. I would like to see some research on developing "best practices" for Holocaust and genocide education, so we know how to present it in a way that can do as much good as possible.

I would also like to see this education happen in other countries, including Africa and Asia, both places that have been affected by genocides that occurred after the Holocaust. Unfortunately, many countries in the Middle East have a history of denying that the Holocaust ever happened or downplaying its deadliness, a version of state-sponsored antisemitism. This lack of education and information makes the area's people easy targets for antisemitic conspiracy theories.[13] One source of light is the recent founding of the Manara Center in the United Arab Emirates, named after the Arabic word for "source of light." The center was established as a partnership between the UAE and the ADL "to help implement key educational programming . . . priorities will include forging relationships with universities across the Middle East and Southeast Asia to promote peace and prosperity through coexistence around the world, with specific trainings designed for university students and young learners."[14] I hope to see more efforts like this to help reduce hate and extremism globally.

So let us spread the light of knowledge through education to dispel the darkness of ignorance. Education is a powerful tool to open the minds, souls, and hearts of the young, so that future generations never forget the damage, violence, and heartbreak that hate and intolerance visit upon the world.

8

The Jewish People's Connection to Israel

The Jewish People are connected to Jews around the world through our common faith, language, history, and our connection to our ancient homeland, Israel. Our liturgy, since the time of the destruction of the temple in Jerusalem in 70 CE, has focused, in part, on our hope of returning to Zion, the land given to us through God's covenant with our ancestors, where our religious tradition was first developed and where our Holy Temple was built thousands of years ago. Every *Shabbat* (our weekly holy day, Saturday) and at every daily religious service (three times each day) we pray for our return to Jerusalem, our holy city, and for peace in the land of Israel, and we have done so for millennia. The land of our ancestors is central to our faith.

* * *

Many years ago, in the early 1950s, I had an extraordinary experience visiting Israel for the first time in my life. I was on a trip organized by the Bureau of Jewish Education in New York City for principals and teachers who wanted to learn more about Israel. We flew together to Tel Aviv, and when we landed, I knelt and kissed the ground with tears of joy at having the merit to stand on the

*land of our ancestors. It was a moment of exultation, and I felt my heart beating
with happiness! As we entered Jerusalem, we joyfully recited the* Shehecheyanu
*prayer, "Praised are you, our God, who grants us life, sustains us, and enables us
to reach this day." The State of Israel was so new that hotels had not yet been built,
so we were assigned to lodge with families. As I was one of the youngest members
of the group, I was placed with a family who provided space for me in their
basement. There was no toilet, and I entered the space through a hole outside.
But I was young and so happy to finally be in Israel that even the dark basement
was fine by me. As you know, I have had some experience with living in difficult
surroundings, including holes in the ground. Of course, this was different—I was
happy and unafraid. I felt protected.*

*While in Israel, I was able to meet two sisters and a brother of my beloved
mother for the first time. All the hugging and kissing brought tears to my eyes
again. These family members had moved to the land of Israel before the Holocaust
and so were spared its horrors. We cried together about what the Nazis had done
to my mother, brothers, and sister. Telling them my story was very emotional for
me, but I thanked God that they had avoided this experience and that we were
all alive and meeting in Israel.*

*The curriculum for our trip required us to visit important places in the Bible.
Every location was so meaningful to me. At the Dead Sea, I learned many things
about the salty water. We planted trees to help the desert bloom. I saw the Dead
Sea Scrolls, and they showed me a window into all aspects of Jewish life in this
land from two thousand years ago. I visited the Temple Mount and prayed at
the* Kotel *(the location of our ancient first and second temples that were mostly
destroyed, first by the Babylonians in 586 BCE and again by the Romans in 70
CE and upon which Muslim holy sites were erected in the seventh century CE).
In our tradition, we write prayers on small pieces of paper and place them in
the crevices between the stones of this ancient edifice. It filled my heart with joy
to pray at this most holy of places, where my ancestors had prayed so long ago.
Every day was educational and meaningful and imbued with holiness. Walking*

the paths walked by my people for thousands of years stirred my soul. The stories of the Bible came alive in new ways. I felt the holiness of my spiritual home surround me wherever I went.

I could feel the collective soul of the Jewish People in this place and was overwhelmed with emotion at what I had been through, what I had lost, and at finally having a place where the Jewish People could live fully, openly, proudly, and freely. Yad Vashem, the memorial to those murdered in the Holocaust, opened in 1953, so, of course, we paid a visit there. I found a record of my town in the museum with an inscription that said only two Jewish children made it through the Holocaust alive. It brought back such powerful memories. It helped us to learn how to teach about the events that led to genocide and the horrors of what happened to so many.

It was such an amazing experience that I vowed to go again, and I did. As a Rabbi, I took thirty-six more trips to Israel with my congregation and many churches from my hometown. I developed great friendships with many pastors, priests, and ministers who joined us with their congregants and parishioners. We shared the powerful experience of following the path that Jesus walked, seeing churches that were important in the life of Jesus, and visiting ancient and modern synagogues, the Kotel, and many other places. I also have taken many educators on these trips. When I would run into people who joined us on our travels, they would greet me and ask, "When can we go again?" I am so pleased that they share some of my feelings about the land of Israel and understand how central and important it is to my life and faith and to the Jewish People.

* * *

Many people, surprisingly, do not realize that the Jewish People have a connection to the land of Israel that goes back a very long time. Let us begin some 4,000 or so years ago. In the Torah, God tells Abraham (Abram at the time) to "go forth from your native land . . . to the land that I will show you."[1] God further tells Abraham, "I will make of you a great nation, and I will bless you. . . . And all the families of the earth shall bless themselves by you."[2] When Abraham arrives in the land of Canaan, God appears and says to him, "I will assign this land to your offspring."[3] This is a seminal moment for the Jewish People; from this point forward, we are inextricably connected to the land God promised to Abraham, the land of Israel.

Two chapters later, Abraham/*Abram* is referred to as "*ha-ivri*"[4] which is commonly translated as "the Hebrew." There are many interpretations as to the derivation of this name, Abraham the Hebrew. In one, it is suggested that the name comes from *Eber*, the name of Noah's grandson,[5] suggesting the relationship between Noah and Abraham. In another, it is connected to the Hebrew word "*eiver*" which means beyond, as in Abraham came from someplace beyond the Euphrates River (in modern-day Iraq). A third understanding refers to the new spiritual direction of Abraham, beyond what came before and toward monotheism, leaving the rest of the world behind, on the other side, where idols are worshiped.[6] Still others suggest that the term *ha-ivri* means "the other," signifying Abraham's status as different from the majority.[7] Whatever the interpretations, Abraham the Hebrew established the Jewish People's presence in the land of Israel and gave its language a new name.

Israel is the land where our forefather Isaac is taken by Abraham to Mount Moriah and is spared sacrifice by God's intervention.[8] This is another place where Abraham, following God's directions, is breaking from the past, where human sacrifice was the accepted norm, as it was in other ancient Near Eastern communities. Our tradition also tells us that Mount Moriah is the location where the Holy Temple is later built.[9]

The land of Israel is again promised by God to our ancestor Jacob when God says to him, "I am the Lord, the God of your father Abraham and the God of Isaac; the ground on which you are lying I will assign to you and your offspring. . . . I will protect you wherever you go and will bring you back to this land."[10] It is at this moment that Jacob realizes God is in this place. It is here that he tends his flock and raises his family, who will become the twelve tribes of Israel and live in this land. It is on the banks of the Jabbok, a tributary to the Jordan River, that Jacob struggles with beings human and divine and earns a new name, *Israel*.[11]

Israel is also the Promised Land to which Moses later led the people from Egyptian bondage. Before entering the land, Moses says to Joshua: "Be strong and resolute, for it is you who shall go with this people into the land that the Lord swore to their fathers to give them and it is you who shall apportion it to them."[12] After Moses dies, the Almighty says to Joshua,

> Prepare to cross the Jordan, together with all this people, into the land that I am giving to the Israelites. Every spot on which your foot treads I give to you, as I promised to Moses. Your territory shall extend from the wilderness and the Lebanon to the Great River, the River Euphrates . . . and up to the Mediterranean Sea on the west.[13]

Joshua did as he was commanded and led the twelve tribes of Israel into the land.

The first reference to what becomes the holy city of Jerusalem occurs in the Torah when Abraham is greeted by Melchizedek, who is identified as the king of "*Shalem*" or Salem.[14] The word *Shalem* means "whole" or "complete." The word "*shalom*" comes from the same root as *Shalem* and means peace. When we feel whole and complete, when we feel unity with God and with others, we have peace/*shalom*. The sages teach that *shalom* is, in fact, another name for the Almighty, so Jerusalem is named as a place where we feel God's presence in peace. Tradition tells us that Abraham later added what would become the prefix "Jeru-," or in Hebrew "*yireh*," meaning "God will see," to the city's name, resulting in the word *yireh-shalem* or Jerusalem,[15] indicating again that this holy city hosts God's presence. Jews today and for centuries have daily prayed that God will see peace in our holy city, Jerusalem.

Jerusalem was also the place where King David based his rule of the land of Israel, at which time the city was also referred to as "*Tzion*," or Zion, after the name of Mount Zion (previously called Mount Moriah) upon which it was located.[16] Many Psalms attributed to King David reference the beauty and centrality of Zion to our faith. Solomon, whose name (*Shlomo*) derives from the word Shalem, later built the first Holy Temple in Jerusalem/Zion around 950 BCE with the aspiration that it would be a place where peace would be seen.

Since the fall of the Second Temple in Jerusalem/Zion in 70 CE, we Jews have prayed for our homeland and our return to Zion and the land of Israel. In the *Amidah*, we ask, among many other petitions, that God gather us together and return us from exile, that God return to and protect Jerusalem, and that we rebuild Zion and the holy city. It is traditional to say this prayer facing the land of Israel. Throughout history, when we have suffered as a tiny minority in so many other nations, we have longed for the return to our ancestral land, which we yearn for as a holy place of safety and peace. Certainly, for many Jews who were fortunate enough to escape the terrors of the Holocaust, our ancient homeland became a place of refuge.

Our holy texts and liturgy are full of references to Israel, Jerusalem, and Zion and have been for millennia. In the *Siddur*, or prayer book, we ask for peace for ourselves and "for all Israel," meaning the people of Israel, the descendants of our forefather Jacob, whose home was the land promised by God (Mourner's *Kaddish, Hatzi Kaddish, Kaddish Shalem*). When we take out the Torah for services, we say the "Torah shall come from Zion, the word of God from Jerusalem. Praised is God who gave the Torah to Israel in holiness"[17] and ask, "May God favor the remnant of His people Israel."[18] In the blessings after the *haftarah* (a weekly reading from the prophets), we pray that the Almighty will "show compassion for Zion, the fount of our existence . . . praised are you Adonai, who brings joy to Zion."[19] Our weekday morning prayers include asking God to "withhold your wrath from your city Jerusalem," "watch over the city which bears your name," and "gather our exiles from the four corners of the earth." Even the *Shema*, a twice-daily prayer proclaiming the oneness and wholeness of God that we hope is on our lips as we die, references Israel.

Many of our holidays also reflect our love and yearning for our homeland. Hanukkah celebrates a victory over an invading ruler who desecrated the Holy Temple and prevented the practice of our faith in our homeland. On *Tisha B'Av*, we mourn the destruction of the Holy Temple in Jerusalem/Zion. On Passover, we celebrate our freedom from enslavement and our return to the Promised Land. We end every Passover Seder with the words, "Next year in Jerusalem."

Israel has been the eternal home of the Jewish People in every age, and Jerusalem/Zion is our holy city. Wherever Jews migrated or were forcibly exiled to outside of the land, wherever we ended up in the world, we have always prayed for our ancient homeland and Holy Temple. Despite being conquered, exiled, becoming refugees, and being a targeted minority throughout the world and throughout time, there has always been a remnant of the Jewish People who remained in the land. Sometimes the community was larger, and sometimes it was smaller; sometimes these Jews had to hide their faith to be safe, and other times they could freely express it. All my life I have prayed and yearned for my People's return to our ancient homeland. Every time I visited this majestic place that generations of my family sought, I was overwhelmed with gratitude. For me and most Jews, Israel is inextricably intertwined with all that makes me Jewish, it factors into all of the holy texts I have spent a lifetime studying; it has been a part of my daily worship for my entire life; it is the source of my faith, my history, and my sacred language. My love for the land of Israel is integral to who I am.

Because I lived through the most vile expression of antisemitism that the world has seen, witnessing the murder of my friends, family members, and neighbors by a regime that believed Jews should be eradicated from the earth, being able to travel to my homeland is meaningful to me. Until 1948, when the State of Israel was created, the Jewish People had been refugees in exile around the world. Like any people we have always wanted to live in peace and security wherever we were, including as a minority in countries around the world. Our reality, however, has been one of limited rights and freedoms, persecution, expulsion, murder, and genocide. It is my dream that Jews can live in peace and freedom in our ancestral homeland as well as in any other land on earth.

When I hear someone criticize the policies of the modern-day government of Israel, I am always interested to hear their thoughts. But when people advocate for the destruction of Israel and its people and say it has no right to exist, I interpret these ideas as hurtful and hateful. Any argument that Jews are not welcome because they are Jews is, by its nature, antisemitic.

When asked when anti-Israel activity is antisemitism, Ambassador Deborah Lipstadt said:

I'm often asked to explain the difference between anti-Zionism and antisemitism. I used to go through a long explanation, threading the needle, explaining that criticism of Israeli policy isn't antisemitism, that's democracy. Now I just say, you're asking the wrong person. Go ask the person who defaced the Holocaust memorial in Paris or the person who firebombed the synagogue in Montreal. They're making the connection themselves.[20]

When someone uses violence against Jews or Jewish institutions around the world because they hate Israel, that is antisemitism. Non-state entities such as Hamas, Hezbollah, and others, recognized around the world as terrorist organizations, call for the destruction of Israel and the killing of Jews wherever they may be, deny the Holocaust, and widely promote anti-Jewish conspiracy theories.[21] Israel is the only nation on earth that is regularly and overtly threatened with extinction. This is antisemitism, full stop.

Those of us with ancient and long-standing ties to this Holy Land are brothers and sisters, and I look forward to the day when we can live as such.

9

Building Community

Community is essential in the fight against antisemitism and all forms of hate. Participating in and cultivating a vibrant Jewish community gives us a place of belonging, safety, and home. It also shows the world that we value our shared ancestry, history, culture, language, and faith. Cultivating community beyond our own is also essential. Sharing our community with others demystifies it, helps them to understand it, and lets them see how much we have in common. It allows us to learn from others and stop antisemitism before it has a chance to grow beyond ignorance or misunderstanding into something more dangerous. Befriending and assisting those in other communities also helps us to better understand the concerns and issues facing others and to support them whenever possible. In doing so, we become more empathetic and compassionate and actively work toward repairing the world.

A Story from the Torah

Sh'mot or Exodus, the second book of the Torah, is about the birth of a nation. It includes the story of the Israelites' sojourn in Egypt, their enslavement, Pharaoh's ruling calling for the murder of all male Jewish children, the Ten Plagues, the Exodus, the miracle of the journey through the sea, and the covenant at Mount Sinai. All these things would become part of the Jewish

People's collective memory. But the sanctuary or *Mishkan* that is also part of this story surely belongs to the book of *Vayikra* or Leviticus, known as *Torat Kohanim*, the book of priestly things. It seems to have no connection with *Sh'mot*/Exodus whatsoever. So why is it included here?

The answer, I believe, is profound and has to do with the deep human need to be part of something bigger than oneself, to build and be part of a community.

* * *

The biblical story from Bereishit *to* Sh'mot, *Genesis to Exodus, is about the evolution from individuals to a family and eventually to a nation. When the Israelites entered Egypt, they were a single extended family. By the time they left Egypt, they had become a sizable People, divided into twelve tribes plus an amorphous collection of followers and fellow travelers known as the* erev rav, *the "mixed multitude."*

They were united by fate. All were people whom the Pharaoh distrusted and enslaved. The Israelites now had a common enemy. Beyond that, they had a shared history in the patriarchs, matriarchs, and their God. But what was to prove difficult, almost impossible, was to get them to share responsibility for the future.

Everything we read in Sh'mot *tells us that, as is so often the case among people long deprived of freedom, the Israelites were passive and they were easily moved to complain. The two often go together. They expected someone else, Moses or God, to provide them with food and water, lead them to safety, and take them to the Promised Land.*

At every setback, they complained. They complained about a lack of water, and when they were given water, they complained that it was bitter. Then there was no food, and when food was provided, they complained that it was not as good as what they had while enslaved.

Soon, Moses himself is saying:

What am I to do with these people? They are almost ready to stone me. (Exod. 17:4)

By now God has performed signs and wonders on the people's behalf, taken them out of Egypt, divided the sea for them, given them water from a rock and manna from heaven, and still they do not cohere as a nation. They are a group of individuals, unwilling or unable to take responsibility, to act collectively.

And now God does the single greatest act in history. He appears in a revelation at Mount Sinai, the only time in history that God has appeared to an entire people, and the people tremble.

A mere forty days later, the people have forgotten this experience and begin to make a Golden Calf, a prohibited idol. If miracles, the division of the sea, and the revelation at Mount Sinai fail to transform the Israelites, what will?

That is when God does the most unexpected thing. He says to Moses: speak to the people and tell them to contribute, to give something of their own, be it gold or silver or bronze, be it wool or animal skin, be it oil or incense, or their skill or their time, and get them to build something together—a symbolic home for My Presence, a Tabernacle. It doesn't need to be large or grand or permanent. Get them to make something, to become builders. Get them to give so they can create something together.

Moses does so. And the people respond. They respond so generously that Moses is told, "The people are bringing more than enough for doing the work the Lord commanded to be done,"[1] and Moses has to ask them to stop.

During the entire time the Tabernacle was being constructed, there were no complaints, rebellions, or dissent. Where all the signs and wonders failed, the communal effort of constructing the Tabernacle succeeded. It transformed the people, turning them into a cohesive group. It gave them a sense of responsibility, purpose, and identity.

* * *

In this context, the story of building the *Mishkan,* or Tabernacle, is the essential element in the birth of this nation. No wonder it is told at length; no surprise, then, that it appears in the book of Exodus.

The *Mishkan* did not last forever, but the lesson it taught did. It is not what God does for us that transforms us, but what we do for God. When we build something together, it becomes meaningful and has value, and we all become committed to its success.

Constructing the *Mishkan* was a call to the Jewish People to create community and holy space wherever they were. For a nation destined to wander, the portable *Mishkan* was the secret to our survival when it eventually became the synagogue (a word of Greek origin), which in Hebrew is *beit knesset,* meaning a house of gathering.

A community is essential for spiritual life. Our holiest prayers require a gathering of ten people, a *minyan,* to be together. When we celebrate and when we mourn, we do so as a community. Even when we confess and atone, as we do on the holiest of days, *Yom Kippur,* we do it collectively. The Jewish tradition before God is a relationship of we and Thou, as much as it is between I and Thou.

The *Mishkan* was how the Jewish People started building community, and it is this community that has enabled us, through the millennia, to stand against the most violent and destructive expressions of antisemitism and survive. We learned that what we can create together will be greater than anything that we create alone.

The verse commanding us to build the *Mishkan* says:

"*Ve'asu li mikdash ve'shachanti be'tocham,*" in English, "They shall make a sanctuary for Me, and I will dwell within them."[2] The verse might have said "I will dwell within **it**" not "I will dwell within **them**." But it doesn't. What the Torah teaches us in this verse is that *Hashem* lies deep inside each of us and in the communities that we build together.

Responding to a Call from the Community

One of my roles and privileges as a Rabbi has been to act as a chaplain to the Connecticut State Police. In this role, I have been available to local police as well, including in Hartford and Bloomfield. Of course, I have given blessings and provided counseling to the officers and their wives as a chaplain, and I have also participated in many ride-alongs with local law enforcement and provided my services in the field as needed.

Several years ago I was in my office at Beth Hillel synagogue in Bloomfield working late at night on a sermon. It was in the winter and during the eight nights of Hanukkah. I had the menorah on the windowsill and five candles provided a warming glow while I wrote at my desk. The phone rang, and when I picked up the receiver, it was the Chief of Police for Hartford on the other end. He apologized for the lateness of the call and explained that they had a young woman at the station who had been the victim of a sexual assault. She was a Christian but had specifically asked to see a rabbi rather than a priest or minister, and I was the only chaplain who was a rabbi. "Would you be willing to come and speak with her?" the chief asked me.

I hesitated for a moment. It was late. I hadn't finished my sermon and I was eager get home to my family. But this young woman had just experienced something traumatic and had asked for my help. I know what it is like to live through something horrific and feel that no one is there to help, so I put aside my thoughts of home and quickly gathered my coat and car keys.

When I arrived at the station, I spoke to the chief and was taken to the young victim. I introduced myself as Rabbi Chaplain and asked for her first name only. I did not ask her about her faith; it did not make any difference; she was a human being. She was frightened and in pain, and I needed to help her. We spoke of her experience, how traumatic it was, and that she was alive and not alone. She was also afraid of what people might say or think about her, and I did what I could to reassure her. We talked for a long time, and by the end of it, she was a renewed person. I suggested that she go to the hospital, and I called her family. I promised her that I would visit her at the hospital, and I did. She thanked me graciously and even smiled when I said goodbye. I wished her well and gave her my phone number if she ever needed my help.

About three hours later I drove back to Beth Hillel. It was very late, but I knew I wouldn't be able to sleep. When I entered my office, intending to finish the work on my sermon, I immediately smelled smoke in the air. I rushed toward the window and saw that my menorah had fallen and was ready to catch the carpet on fire. I quickly stamped it out and thanked God that I had arrived in time to prevent a disaster. Then I thought to myself, "Why is the menorah on the ground?"

I took a moment to look around, and my eyes were drawn to the window where the Hanukkah menorah had been sitting and was shocked to see there was a bullet hole in the glass. I admit that I was frightened. I scanned my office and realized that the bullet was lodged in a painting of the Vilna Gaon, my favorite rabbi. This painting hung on the wall right behind my desk. Had I been in my chair, as I was earlier, had I not been called away, had a Christian girl not asked for my help, and had I not responded to that cry, I would have been hit by that bullet.

* * *

This story has always stayed with me because it showed me, with a miracle, the importance of working and supporting my community. I was proudly celebrating Hanukkah, displaying the candles in my window, and working on a sermon to motivate and support my congregation. At the same time, this story showed me the importance of caring beyond my community and working toward *tikkun olam* in the wider world. I responded to the call from the police and attended to the needs of a young person dealing with trauma. It is not an exaggeration to say that working to build the Jewish community and responding to the needs of the wider community literally saved my synagogue and my life. I cannot know the intention of the person who shot at my synagogue, but the impact felt like violence directed at me and my congregation as Jews. It felt like antisemitism. Not only did taking the time to help someone outside of my community save my life, it also showed me the power of fighting hate through building bridges.

I believe that committing to cultivating the Jewish community and engaging with communities beyond our own is critical to saving our collective lives and fighting hate and antisemitism. Building strong Jewish communities is essential to providing a place to practice our faith in safety, to learn, to support each other in times of need, and to celebrate our successes. While it may not seem obvious, indeed, we can more effectively fight antisemitism if we first have a cohesive community. When we live in the world with pride in our community, we can then share our knowledge, culture, faith, and experiences with other communities to increase peace and understanding. We can also be more present to learn from and understand others and to engage in mutual support.

Scripture teaches us that, *"vi-ahavta l'reacha kamocho,"* "you shall love your neighbor as you love yourself."[3] This is a very difficult commandment to observe. The effort to live up to this mitzvah is so hard that some have suggested that we should be glad if we could get even halfway there. It is easy to love humankind, but to love your neighbor, the one who parks in your spot, doesn't clean up after her dog, plays loud music at night, or never has a friendly greeting, is a challenge. Reaching out to other faith traditions and other groups with whom we share common bonds is also part of fulfilling this commandment, even when it is challenging.

In addition to loving our neighbors, we are commanded to *"hocheach tochiach et amitecha,"*[4] chastise your neighbor when you see him or her doing something wrong. This might be even harder to do effectively. When you criticize someone, they often become defensive or even hostile. The sages even say that anyone who can protest against the wrongdoings of his household and does not do so is liable for them. This extends to the wrongdoings of one's community and even of one's country. Both loving our neighbors, Jewish and non-Jewish, and addressing their wrongs are part of our obligations in building community. This is especially true when it comes to hateful attitudes and ideas; we must challenge them in our community, and we must also help other communities understand when their attitudes or words are antisemitic or otherwise bigoted.

These can both be hard to do. The wisdom of Rabbi Shlomo Riskin of Efrat may be able to guide us. He focused on respect. If someone does something offensive to you, the most effective way to help that person realize their wrong is by showing kindness and sensitivity.

Rabbi Riskin tells this story:

* * *

I had a friend who was a distinguished Jewish educator in Jerusalem. This man was invited, a year in advance, to speak at the graduation ceremonies of a high school in Israel. Shortly before the ceremony, my friend became seriously ill and was hospitalized. He came home from the hospital greatly weakened, so his wife called the principal, explained the situation, and asked if her husband could be excused from the speaking engagement.

The principal was adamant that he come and speak. "It would be a desecration of God's name if you do not show up! We have announced your name! You must come, even if you have to crawl on all fours to get here," he said, not even offering to send a car or pay for a taxi.

In light of this response, my friend insisted on meeting his obligation, despite his wife's protestations. Along the way, he wondered how his beloved grandfather would have taught the principal that he had behaved with insensitivity. He decided that his grandfather would have tried to teach this man how to behave by giving him an example of proper conduct.

And so, when he was called on to speak, my friend gave a brief introduction. He added that he wanted to give a special word of thanks to the principal of the school who had invited him to speak. He said that this principal, when he learned that my friend was ill, called to suggest that he stay home. And then, when my friend "insisted" on coming, the principal offered to send a car. And therefore, my friend said, it was only proper to thank him for his sensitivity and his consideration before giving the commencement address.

The audience was so impressed that they gave the principal a standing ovation. The next day, the principal called to apologize and to thank my friend for having taught him a most important lesson in such a gentle way.

* * *

This man did his best to love his neighbor and addressed a wrong without publicly shaming, embarrassing, or humiliating him. He exercised care, diplomacy, and delicacy in his rebuke. I feel that the great moral of the story is to resist sinking to the level of those who hurt us or treat us disrespectfully. Patience and compassion are important, even with those who treat us badly. Treating everyone with dignity, as the Torah teaches us, is a first step toward reducing hatred in our community and in the world beyond. This practice of loving our neighbors and helping them to understand their wrongs is a critical component in fighting antisemitism, which so often is based on ignorance or belief in conspiracy theories. Loving your neighbor is not just a utopian idea. It is a commandment and a goal—it is a standard to hold ourselves to. Who knows? We might just be able to tilt the balance between good and evil and make this a world of peace as it ought to be.

When I answered the call to help a victim of sexual violence, I had the opportunity to love my neighbor and, I hope, to bring more peace into the world. Maybe my words of comfort have been remembered, and maybe the fact that a rabbi delivered them helps this young woman to speak out against antisemitism when she sees it. I will never know, but my actions that night at least make this possible. Unfortunately, we often do not view people who are far away or are different from us as fellow human beings; they can easily become objects of lies and hate. Engaging across communities makes it harder for this to happen. As author Emmanuel Acho notes, "proximity breeds care, and distance breeds fear."[5]

The commandments to love our neighbor and to address wrongs are individual and communal responsibilities. I strongly believe that people have a deep need to belong. We have a drive to connect, to be social, and to be part of relationships and larger groups. This need is very powerful and shapes many aspects of our thoughts, emotions, and behavior.

The *Mishnah Pirkei Avot* addresses the importance of community. In it, the sage Hillel admonishes us, "Do not separate yourself from the community."[6] Scholars and mystics sometimes desire to remove themselves from society to learn deeply and spend time in reflection and introspection. People, they feel, are a distraction from their lofty goals. Rabbi Shem Tov, in commenting on Hillel's statement, believes that people are social by nature and that we grow and develop, physically, spiritually, and intellectually, with the help of others and society more broadly. The rabbis knew that healthy social relationships increase our self-awareness, improve both individuals and the larger community, and prevent bad behavior.

Hillel goes on to add, "And do not judge your fellow man until you have reached his place."[7] The character Atticus Finch in the novel *To Kill a Mockingbird* famously restated this idea when he suggested that to know another person, you must try to see the world from their point of view. This is how we develop empathy for others, trying to get inside their skin and see what life is like for them. Community helps us do this—first through connections and understanding within our groups and then in the wider world. This is an essential part of reducing hate and antisemitism. When we are active in building healthy communities, we learn more about what others experience, and they in turn learn what we have been through. We can share and learn from each other to make it easier to walk in each other's shoes and see life from another perspective. This way, we avoid an overly judgmental stance toward others and have the chance to build love and cohesion.

Rabbi Hillel also addresses the tension between personal and social responsibility when he asks, "If I am not for myself, who will be for me, but if I am only for myself, who am I?"[8] Here he recognizes the need for individual pursuits (he, of course, prioritizes learning) but also acknowledges that we cannot be isolated from others. And doing so renders our learning partial and incomplete. He closes with, "If not now, when?" In his wisdom, he encourages us not to procrastinate in taking advantage of all opportunities to grow, including and especially in the company of and in connecting with others.

In a diverse democratic system, peaceful coexistence is a must. To live in friendship, we must be united and not live in fear or run away from our obligations to participate in society. Closing our doors and hiding inside will not help us; we must continue to be engaged with other groups and faiths in our communities. Building community both reinforces shared values and promotes social cohesion and cooperation. Deepening our connections with our Jewish community and beyond promotes belonging, security, and connectedness.

We must learn the lesson of Jonah the Prophet. God asked Jonah to go to Nineveh (a city that, if it existed today, would be located across the Tigris River from Mosul, Iraq) and warn the many people there, regardless of their faith or identity, of God's judgment on them. Instead, Jonah ran away from his responsibility, boarded a ship, and endured a mighty storm sent by God. To save the sailors on the ship from the storm, Jonah asked that they cast him overboard, as he knew that the storm was brought on by God's anger at Jonah's refusal to warn the people of Nineveh. The sailors threw Jonah into the sea, and he found refuge in the belly of a huge fish for three days until, at God's request, the fish spit Jonah up onto the shore. Now Jonah went to Nineveh and warned the people of the impending catastrophe, and everyone repented. The community was saved.

Jonah could not run away or hide from God, and he was punished for trying to avoid his responsibility. We too must not run away from our responsibility to save our community. We must have the courage to challenge ourselves to work together, to show kindness and love, to ease pain, and to help broken lives heal—to engage in *tikkun olam*. We must do this for our own community as well as our neighbors.

The US National Strategy to Counter Antisemitism states:

> [T]argeted communities are often too siloed in their experiences of hate and attempts to combat it. Antisemitism and other forms of hate do not operate in isolation from each other; nor should the communities they target. Increasing space for deeper awareness, shared empathy, and action across communities is critical to preventing hate and building resilience in the face of rising antisemitic and other hate-motivated violence. . . . A diversity of voices and actors signals that antisemitism is not just a problem for Jews, but for all. At the same time, it is crucial that Jewish communities continue to speak out and intensify their efforts against other forms of hate that afflict so many different communities in America and support other communities when they are targeted.[9]

It means a lot to me that when the Jewish community experiences antisemitism, non-Jews reach out and express concern about me, my community, and the level of hate. It shows me that people are thinking about me and my community, and I let them know that I appreciate their kindness. We must do the same and reach out to our friends, especially those in other marginalized communities, to support them when their community is under fire.

We can work with other groups to advocate with local, state, and federal elected officials for laws, policies, and programs that help fight hatred of all kinds, including that targeting the Jewish community. When we advocate on issues that will reduce hate and antisemitism, our neighbors of other backgrounds will benefit as well. For example, federal and state programs provide grants to increase the security of targeted houses of worship, religious institutions, and nonprofits. These grants help synagogues, mosques, churches, and others have the funds to make their institutions more secure and safe from violence or attack. When we advocate for these policies, we all benefit.

If we teach or coach children, we can show them how to love their neighbor and correct wrongs by always taking the time to address any bigoted comments against Jews or any other group that we hear them utter. This is also true in our interactions with adults.

In our places of work, we can respect that Jewish employees may have different needs because of keeping kosher, observing Shabbat, and taking time for holidays that are not in the Christian calendar. The same may be true for employees of other faith traditions. We can learn from each other and operate from a place of mutual respect.

We can engage in or develop collaborative service projects that include multi-faith and intergroup coalitions that benefit the entire community. This could include projects that involve youth groups from a variety of religious communities and could even include social and educational efforts.

Clergy of all kinds can educate themselves about the various ways that antisemitism is expressed and call it out whenever it is found within their communities. And Jewish faith leaders should call out hateful speech within the Jewish community.

We must strive to create connections within our community and across communities to prevent hate and division from seeping in. We Jews have been the target of much animosity and division, and we have suffered greatly when others have not seen us as human and failed to acknowledge our inherent goodness. We must not let an antisemite destroy us through baseless hatred. We must rebuild ourselves and others through baseless love.

Conclusion and Call to Action

I have been through so much in the many years of my life, and so many times when it seemed like the end was in sight, faith and perseverance led me from the darkness into the light.

* * *

In the late afternoon on the day my second son, Alan, was born, the excellent doctor who helped my wife, Ruth, with the delivery came to see me in the hospital waiting room. He told me in no uncertain terms, "Your boy will not make it through the night. His lungs are not open and functioning." He continued, "I know that you are a Rabbi and the only thing that might help him now is prayer." He was adamant that there was nothing more that could be done.

I was devastated. Yet I thanked him for being frank with me and asked him not to tell Ruth. When I went home that night, I began to pray. I prayed with fear and begged God not to take my son away. I prayed through the whole night, and when I saw the light of the sun coming over the horizon, a feeling of hope came over me. I felt my fear leave me, and I felt that God might hear my prayers and let Alan live. With this sense of possibility and hopefulness coursing through me, I ran to Mount Sinai Hospital. When I rushed in, I saw that the doctor was there. He looked up and said to me, "Your prayers did something. His lungs just opened and had they not opened within a few minutes, he would have died."

I thank God for returning my son from death to life. I am blessed with the strong faith that God, my family, and my community instilled in me. I learned yet again that even if the knife is at your throat, do not give up. This is what my experiences in the Holocaust and in my long life since then have taught me.

* * *

We must never give up in our efforts to bring peace into our world. We must find the stamina to fight the darkness that is hate and antisemitism, the shadows cast by ignorance, and the confusion and opacity of conspiracy theories. We must each bring the light of education, wisdom, love, compassion, and hope to dispel this darkness.

Ambassador Deborah Lipstadt notes that "many people, organizations, and institutions, including those who valiantly fight other prejudices with all their hearts and might, fail to see antisemitism as a serious danger."[1] But I know from experience that it *is* a serious danger. We must, all of us, engage in the effort to counter antisemitism because, "Protecting the Jewish community from antisemitism is essential to our broader fight against all forms of hate, bigotry, and bias—and to our broader vision of a thriving, inclusive, and diverse democracy. . . . We must confront antisemitism early and aggressively whenever and wherever it emerges from the darkness."[2]

To do this better, we, Jews and non-Jews alike, can aspire toward a more thorough understanding of what antisemitism is and how it is expressed today. We can call it out when we see it, in the same way that we condemn racism and other forms of hate when we see them. Becoming familiar with the long history of antisemitism will help all of us to do this. Looking to this history, we can better understand the present and learn that acting early when antisemitic bias is expressed in words, attitudes, and ideas, before it evolves into violence, is extremely important. Knowing the history of the Jewish People illuminates how easily attitudes can become murderous. We must also be sensitive to the fact that leaders have historically amplified antisemitism and other forms of hate for personal or political gain and in many countries today continue to do the same.

Understanding antisemitism includes knowing more about the Jewish People too. We are not only a religion; we have a shared ancestry and history, an ancient and sacred language, diverse cultures that are connected across the globe, and an ancestral homeland. We come in every color, political persuasion, gender, and gender identity that humanity displays and live on every continent. We are rich and we are poor; we are left-wing, centrist, and right-wing; we are religiously observant and atheists. And not one of us is exactly like the other. But, like our ancestor, Jacob/Israel, we all wrestle with beings both human and divine. And not one of us should be ostracized, demeaned, devalued, or harmed because we identify as Jewish.

Our history, faith, and traditions are rich and meaningful, and we take pride in who we are and what our People have contributed to the world. Our scripture, holidays, and history acknowledge the reality of evil and darkness, yet the Almighty has called us to be a "light unto the nations," and many of us take this responsibility seriously. Our faith requires us to pursue justice, peace, and understanding, and we believe in the inherent goodness of human beings and that we all have the potential to improve and evolve. Every synagogue service includes a prayer for peace.

I know that not everyone shares the deep faith that I have. But I do know that faith has undergirded my life and saved me time and again because it meant I always had hope. I encourage everyone to work on developing their faith, whatever it might be. Maybe it's faith in the traditional religious sense, or maybe it's faith in the resilience and wonder of the natural world, or maybe it is faith in the transformative power of compassion, empathy, and love. Faith gives us hope, and in the fight against hatred, we always need hope. In my experience, faith allows the possible to become real.

Friendships also matter in working against hate. They create the potential for goodness and happiness and lead to building peace. Friendships strengthen our communities, and when we reach beyond our communities and make friends across our differences, we can help to prevent resentment, anger, and animosity toward others. Maybe this seems trite, but if you are Jewish and all your friends are Jewish, or you are Christian and all your friends are Christian, you may want to expand your circle. Your life will be richer and give you more opportunities to build bridges of understanding. We cannot correct misinformation, stereotypes, and other biases if we are not talking to each other. Many otherwise good people may believe all kinds of antisemitic things because they have never met a Jew, never had a Jewish friend, never been to a Shabbat dinner or experienced a Jewish holiday. We all can do more to work toward being better friends. This is something every one of us can do to reduce hate and increase understanding.

It requires courage to stand up against hate. Faith and friends can inspire us to find the courage we need in difficult moments. My friend Father Kiely stood up for me, and together we positively affected many lives. And when you do stand up to hate and bias, you never know where the ripples of that action may lead. You may find that the next time you need to stand up in the face of hate, it's easier or that someone you didn't even know was inspired by your courage and felt empowered to pay it forward.

We also need to continue to educate ourselves and our children about the Holocaust and about where unchecked hateful ideas can lead. Evidence shows that learning this can reduce hate and increase understanding. Knowledge and compassion are some of our greatest tools in combating hate. It is never too late to learn; even one who begins their education at the age of ninety can become like Rabbi Akiva, one of the wisest of the ancient Jewish sages. Our young people must be educated about hate, antisemitism, and bias because

the existence of prejudice in any of its forms is a threat to all those who value an inclusive, democratic, and multicultural society. It is axiomatic that if Jews are being targeted with hateful rhetoric and prejudice, other minorities should not feel immune; this is not likely to end with the Jews. And, conversely, if other minority groups are being targeted with hatred and prejudice, Jews should not feel immune: this is not likely to end with these groups either.[3]

Building a stronger Jewish community and building bridges with other communities fight hate the way friendship does, only on a bigger scale. This is how we become allies for others and how others become allies for us. Building community means that we value interaction and take responsibility for one another.

We can be inspired by the prophet's prescription for happiness: "And if you draw out your soul to the hungry and relieve men in misery, the light shall dawn for you in darkness and your dull hours shall be bright as noon."[4] In other words, kindling a light in someone else's life can bring joy into your own life. Doing so within a community expressing shared values is even more powerful.

All of these are ways we can fight hate and antisemitism together, in unity with others. Our strength is magnified when we unite, across our differences, to fight the common enemy that is hate. A Yiddish expression says that when *"tzvey mentchen der driter chapt the hitel,"* when two people argue or fight, a third one catches the hat. When we are divided, especially when so many of our communities are facing hatred, we are all in more danger. Unfortunately, that is what happens when brothers fight each other. Where there is no unity, a third person grabs the hat. We are stronger when we are united against hate; we all have more security and stability. As scripture says, "Have we not all one father? Has not God created us?"[5] Combating antisemitism requires a collective effort from individuals, communities, and organizations. By acting together, we can change history. We must commit to acts of *chesed*, loving-kindness. Despite the darkness of the ancient hatred of antisemitism, we must radiate love and hope. We must strive to become informed, understanding, concerned, committed, and connected, and to act. We must work to usher in a peaceful world. This, in substance, is life's purpose. With acceptance, respect, and connection, *b'yachad nenatzeyach,* together we will triumph.

Call to Action

I know that each of us can commit to doing at least one thing to counter antisemitism and hate and I have identified ways to do so in each chapter. Here are more suggestions:

1. Study history from trusted sources by reading articles or books, watching documentaries, or participating in webinars provided by trusted organizations and not from social media. Learn about the history of antisemitism and the history of the Jewish People.

2. Learn about a faith different from your own, especially one, like Judaism, that is practiced by a small group of people. This is even more important if you are unlikely to meet such a person in your daily life.

3. Share your faith and traditions with others, not to convert them, but to understand others better. Invite a non-Jew to a Shabbat dinner or a Passover Seder or a *bar* or *bat mitzvah*. If you belong to another faith, invite a Jew, Muslim, Hindu, and so on to share in a service project or religious celebration. Be willing to explain your tradition and its meaning to you.

4. Support Jewish communal organizations. This support can be in the form of donations, volunteering, or participating in their initiatives.

5. Support interfaith groups. Again, this support can be in the form of donations, volunteering, or participating in their initiatives.

6. Study Torah, the Bible, and other religious texts on your own or with a group. Better yet, study with others of different faiths. While you will find much that is different, there will be much you have in common.

7. Educate yourself about antisemitism and other prejudices and actively challenge stereotypes. Avoid repeating antisemitic tropes or other prejudicial comments.

8. Speak up against hate speech and discrimination. Encourage respectful dialogue and promote tolerance. Sometimes you may need to gently explain why something is hateful and hurtful.

9. Support legislation and policies that address and prevent antisemitism and other forms of hate and bias. Encourage your government, at every level, to adopt and enforce measures that protect the rights of the Jewish People and prevent harmful discrimination.

10. If you witness or experience antisemitic or hate incidents, report them to the appropriate authorities or organizations that track hate crimes and incidents, including ADL at ADL.org or Secure Community Network at securecommunitynetwork.org/incidentreporting. You can also report to local authorities. In Connecticut, you can report at https://reporthate.ct.gov/. If an incident is not reported, it's as if it never happened. Not every incident is a crime, but reporting every incident matters, even if there is nothing you want done about it. Reporting helps raise awareness, ensures appropriate action is taken, and provides the data that drives policy. Collecting this data helps understand and predict trends and provides the information needed to develop interventions. Remember that hateful words and expressions always precede hateful violence.

11. Read the US National Strategy to Counter Antisemitism from May 2023,[6] This document is only 60 pages long and has over 100 action

items, many of which apply to local governments, private businesses, the arts, education, and sports. I am sure there is one item in this document that you can advocate for or that can inspire a change in your workplace, team, school, or business. Many of these action items apply to all forms of hate. This document is a "blueprint for tackling other forms of bigotry, hate, and bias that fuel toxic divisions in America." Share it widely.

12. Review the US Department of State Global Guidelines for Countering Antisemitism, https://www.state.gov/global-guidelines-for -countering-antisemitism/. This document is only three pages long, but if implemented would help to address antisemitism around the globe, especially in places where the official government policy and education systems continue to include antisemitism. If you ever have an opportunity to advocate for the adoption of its provisions with federal leaders in the United States or with foreign leaders, I hope that you will do so. One of its most important provisions concerns providing truthful and accurate education about the Jewish People and the Holocaust, something that is absent in many nations and greatly contributes to the rise in antisemitism at home and abroad.

13. Share your pride and joy in your heritage with others. Celebrate Jewish American Heritage Month in May.

14. Form a Jewish employee resource group at your workplace and encourage non-Jews to be allies by inviting them to programs.

15. Make sure that an understanding of antisemitism is part of any anti-bias, anti bullying, or diversity, initiative that you participate in or that your workplace, school, or business conducts.

16. I do not use social media or play online games with others, but I do know that in both of these places antisemitism and other forms

of hate run rampant.[7] Using these technologies responsibly, which includes refraining from posting or sharing hateful, conspiracy-laden content, is critical to addressing antisemitism and other forms of hate. These platforms have a global reach that the Nazis could not have imagined, which makes the hate spewed on them so dangerous. Please counter, challenge, and report this hate every time you see it. It is also important to advocate for policies that will reduce online hate and antisemitism. We all must be vigilant about understanding whatever we post online, making sure that it is accurate and does not spread hateful ideas or conspiracy theories. We must also advocate for community guidelines, codes of conduct, and terms of service that do not allow for extremist and hateful content, and these codes, guidelines, and terms must be enforced across all platforms. You can learn more at https://www.adl.org/research-centers/center-technology -society.

Combating antisemitism is an ongoing, every-generation effort and requires active involvement by individuals and communities. We must arm ourselves with all the tools at our disposal: education; understanding history; building community; reaching out in friendship; and using these tools to fight against hatred, bigotry, and ignorance every day. My challenge is not only fighting antisemitism; rather, it is to see human fulfillment where we can live together without hate and scatter seeds of kindness without fear so that all of us can live in wholeness, safety, and peace.

* * *

One evening, I was leading prayers at a shiva *house (a house in mourning), and a woman approached me. She said, "Rabbi, you saved my life." I was dumbfounded. I did not recognize this woman, so I said, "I barely know you!" She then told me that years before, she had come to synagogue one day and listened to my sermon.*

This was at a time when she was suffering from a mental health crisis and felt she had nowhere to turn. She said that my sermon changed her life, made her feel free, and that she would be forever grateful. To this day, I do not know what I said to cause this transformation, but to me, this is a powerful example that when you put goodness out into the world, you can change the future for the better.

In *B'reshit*, or Genesis, we learn at the beginning of creation that, "God said, 'Let there be light'; and there was light. God saw that the light was good, and God separated the light from the darkness."[8] This is our sacred task every day, to separate the light from the darkness. Each of us has an obligation to be a blessing, a light, to the world and to engage with others and act in a way that inspires them to bring light to the darkness.

I have been blessed to see all that God has done for me. The credit belongs to God and my beloved mother, family and teachers. I hope that by reflecting on what the years have taught me, I can share some wisdom to help others navigate hostility and live up to our purpose of bringing peace to our lives and the lives of others. We are commanded to "do justice, love mercy, and walk humbly with thy God."[9] Whether or not you believe in the Almighty, the Divine, the Transcendent, I hope you will join me in doing justice, loving mercy, and walking humbly.

I would like to end with a prayer:

Almighty God, Creator of all humanity:
You have taught us that every human is made in your divine image. That each life is precious and has the capacity for good or evil.
Bless us with the radiant light of thy presence. Help us to turn away from the darkness that is hatred and violence.
Show us your kindness and cause a new light to shine on Zion.
Grant us the knowledge, wisdom, determination, and courage to combat ideologies of hate that motivate acts of evil, prejudice, bigotry, antisemitism, and violence.

Evil actions by those enveloped in darkness challenge us to do the hard work of eradicating prejudice, bigotry, and hatred. May we be supported in this work.

Grant us the insight and determination to work with all people of goodwill until the concepts and teachings that fuel these evil attitudes and acts disappear from the earth.

Bless the work of all people who fight the hateful ideologies of today, even as we remember the atrocities of the past.

We yearn for the vision of your prophet Isaiah that "None shall hurt or destroy in all my holy mountain."

May the knowledge of You, and the rejection of hatred, racism, antisemitism, and all bigotry guide us in the vital work ahead.

May the lessons of my life and the words of this book increase understanding between people, bring light into the darkness, give courage to those who stand up to hatred and not bow to indifference, and increase good in the world.

May we live to see the day when love and justice flow like a mighty stream and peace fills the earth as the waters fill the sea.

May we walk together in harmony and peace forevermore.

Amen.

RESOURCES FOR FURTHER STUDY

Books about Antisemitism

Antisemitism Here and Now by Deborah E. Lipstadt. Penguin Random House, 2019.
It Could Happen Here by Jonathan Greenblatt. Mariner Books, 2022.
People Love Dead Jews by Dara Horn. W.W. Norton & Company, 2022.
The Jew Is Not My Enemy: Unveiling the Myths that Fuel Muslim Anti-Semitism by Tarek Fatah. McClelland and Stewart, 2010.
Uncomfortable Conversations with a Jew by Emanuel Acho and Noa Tishby. Simon Element, 2025.

Memoirs by Those Raised in Hate and Antisemitism

Rising Out of Hatred: The Awakening of a Former White Nationalist by Eli Saslow. Penguin Random House, 2019.
The Fox Hunt by Mohammed Al Samawi. Mariner Books, 2018.
The Gift of Our Wounds by Pardeep Kaleka and Arno Michaelis. St. Martin's Press, 2018.

Articles

ABA Human Rights Magazine-December 2024 Special Issue: Combating Antisemitism. https://www.americanbar.org/groups/crsj/publications/human_rights_magazine _home/combating-antisemitism/.
American Bar Association Resolution 514 Concerning Antisemitism. https://www .americanbar.org/content/dam/aba/directories/policy/midyear-2023/514-midyear -2023.pdf.
"Skin in the Game: How Antisemitism Animates White Nationalism" by Eric Ward. https://politicalresearch.org/2017/06/29/skin-in-the-game-how-antisemitism-animates -white-nationalism.

"Why the Most Educated People in America Still Fall for Antisemitic Lies" by Dara Horn. https://www.theatlantic.com/ideas/archive/2024/02/jewish-anti-semitism-harvard -claudine-gay-zionism/677454/.

Websites

Anti-Defamation League. adl.org.
International Holocaust Remembrance Alliance. https://holocaustremembrance.com.
Museum of Jewish Heritage. mjhnyc.org.
Nexus Document, another working definition of antisemitism as it relates to the connection with Israel. https://nexusproject.us/nexus-resources/the-nexus-document/.
United States Holocaust Memorial Museum. ushmm.org.
Voices of Hope, ctvoicesofhope.org.

US Government Documents

Executive Order on Additional Measures to Combat Antisemitism. https://www .whitehouse.gov/presidential-actions/2025/01/additional-measures-to-combat-anti -semitism/.
The United States National Strategy to Counter Antisemitism. https://www.whitehouse .gov/wp-content/uploads/2023/05/U.S.-National-Strategy-to-Counter-Antisemitism .pdf.
The United States Department of State Global Guidelines for Countering Antisemitism. https://www.state.gov/global-guidelines-for-countering-antisemitism/.

NOTES

Introduction

1 "What is Genocide," Holocaust Encyclopedia, *US Holocaust Memorial Museum.* Available online: https://encyclopedia.ushmm.org/content/en/article/what-is -genocide#origin-of-the-term-genocide-0. (accessed February 2, 2025).

2 Ibid.

3 "Support for Hamas Terror at Anti-Israel Rallies Across the US," The Center on Extremism, *ADL,* October 8, 2023, updated October 14, 2023. Available online: https://www.adl.org/resources/article/support-hamas-terror-anti-israel-rallies-across -us (accessed February 2, 2025); "Anti-Israel Activists Celebrate Hamas Attacks that Have Killed Hundreds of Israelis," The Center on Extremism, *ADL,* October 7, 2023, updated October 14, 2023. Available online: https://www.adl.org/resources/ article/anti-israel-activists-celebrate-hamas-attacks-have-killed-hundreds-israelis (accessed February 2, 2025); "Day of Resistance Toolkit," *National Students for Justice in Palestine,* undated, released in anticipation of October 12, 2023 rallies. Available online: https://dw-wp-production.imgix.net/2023/10/DAY-OF-RESISTANCE -TOOLKIT.pdf (accessed February 2, 2025).

4 Pirkei Avot, Rabban Shimon ben Gamliel, 1:18, Rabbi Hillel 1:12.

5 The Rabbinical Assembly, *Siddur Sim Shalom: For Shabbat and Festivals,* The United Synagogue of Conservative Judaism, New York City, 2005, 148.

6 Midrash Sifrei Numbers.

7 Isa. 42:6.

8 Isa. 41:10.

9 Deut. 31:6.

10 Isa. 54:13.

11 Brachot 64a.

12 Pirkei Avot 2:16.

13 Pirkei Avot 1:14.

Chapter 1

1 Est. 3:6.

2 Est. 3:8.

3 Est. 3:9.

4 Lipstadt, D. E., *Antisemitism Here and Now*, Schocken Books, New York, 2019, 19.

5 Ibid.

6 Goldberg, A., "An Interview with Professor Yehuda Bauer," January 18, 1998, 46. Available online: https://www.yadvashem.org/odot_pdf/microsoft%20word%20-%20 3856.pdf (accessed February 2, 2025).

7 "Working Definition of Antisemitism," *The International Holocaust Remembrance Alliance*, 2016. Available online: https://holocaustremembrance.com/resources/ working-definition-antisemitism (accessed February 2, 2025).

8 Ibid.

9 Ibid.

10 US National Strategy to Counter Antisemitism, 2023. Available online: https:// bidenwhitehouse.archives.gov/wp-content/uploads/2023/05/U.S.-National-Strategy -to-Counter-Antisemitism.pdf (accessed March 11, 2025); Antisemitism Awareness Act of 2023. Available online: https://www.congress.gov/bill/118th-congress/house -bill/6090 (accessed February 2, 2025).

11 "A Closer Look at the Relationship Between Holocaust Knowledge, Education and Antisemitism," The Center for Antisemitism Research, *ADL*, April 14, 2023. Available online: https://www.adl.org/resources/article/closer-look-relationship-between -holocaust-knowledge-education-and-antisemitism (accessed February 2, 2025).

12 "The ADL Global 100 Index of Antisemitism," *ADL*, January 14, 2025. Available online: https://www.adl.org/adl-global-100-index-antisemitism (accessed February 2, 2025).

13 "Blood Libel Accusations Resurface in Wake of Oct. 7," International Affairs, *ADL*, January 26, 2024. Available online: https://www.adl.org/resources/article/blood-libel -accusations-resurface-wake-oct-7 (accessed February 2, 2025).

14 Our Mission, *Connecticut Voices of Hope*. Available online: https://www .ctvoicesofhope.org/about-us/our-mission/ (accessed February 2, 2025).

15 "A Closer Look at the Relationship Between Holocaust Knowledge, Education and Antisemitism," Center for Antisemitism Research, *ADL*, April 14, 2023. Available

online: https://www.adl.org/resources/article/closer-look-relationship-between-holocaust-knowledge-education-and-antisemitism (accessed February 2, 2025).

16 Ibid. Note: This data was collected before October 7, 2023, and may be even higher now.

17 "The Covenant of the Islamic Resistance Movement, Hamas Covenant 1988," August 18, 1988. Available online: https://avalon.law.yale.edu/20th_century/hamas.asp (accessed February 2, 2025).

18 "The Nuremberg Race Laws," The Holocaust Encyclopedia, *US Holocaust Memorial Museum*. Available online: https://encyclopedia.ushmm.org/content/en/article/the-nuremberg-race-laws (accessed February 2, 2025).

19 "Mission and History," *ADL*. Available online: https://www.adl.org/about/mission-and-history (accessed February 2, 2025).

20 "Audit of Antisemitic Incidents," *ADL*. Available online: https://www.adl.org/audit-antisemitic-incidents (accessed February 2, 2025).

21 "Antisemitic Attitudes in America: Conspiracy Theories, Holocaust Education and Other Predictors of Antisemitic Belief," The Center for Antisemitism Research, *ADL*, March 17, 2023. Available online: https://www.adl.org/resources/report/antisemitic-attitudes-america-conspiracy-theories-holocaust-education-and-other (accessed February 2, 2025).

22 Sager, M., "Berlin Police Chief Issues Warning for Jews in City's Arab Neighborhoods," *Newsweek*, November 19, 2024, updated November 20, 2024. Available online: https://www.newsweek.com/jewish-berlin-germany-antisemitism-lgbtq-arab-1988228 (accessed February 2, 2025).

23 "Playing With Hate: How Online Gamers with Diverse Usernames are Treated," Center for Technology and Society, *ADL*, January 16, 2025. Available online: https://www.adl.org/resources/report/playing-hate-how-online-gamers-diverse-identity-usernames-are-treated (accessed February 2, 2025).

24 "Online Hate and Harassment: The American Experience 2024," Center for Technology and Society, *ADL*, June 11, 2024. Available online: https://www.adl.org/resources/report/online-hate-and-harassment-american-experience-2024; "Online Antisemitism: How Tech Platforms Handle Online User Reporting Post 10/7," Center for Technology and Society, *ADL*, September 30, 2024. Available online: https://www.adl.org/resources/report/online-antisemitism-how-tech-platforms-handle-user-reporting-post-107 (accessed February 2, 2025); "AB587 Revisited: How are Online Platforms Complying with California's Newly Mandated Transparency Reporting?" Center for Technology and Society, *ADL*, August 27, 2024. Available online: https://www.adl.org/resources/report/ab587-revisited-how-are-platforms-complying-californias-newly-mandated (accessed February 2, 2025).

Chapter 2

1 Deut. 32:7.

2 Exod. 12:14.

3 Ps. 118.

4 Shaviv, M., "Disraeli Please Come Home," *The Forward*, September 18, 2008. Available online: https://forward.com/culture/14215/disraeli-please-come-home -02534/ (accessed February 2, 2025).

5 "Blood Libel," Holocaust Encyclopedia, *US Holocaust Memorial Museum*. Available online: https://encyclopedia.ushmm.org/content/en/article/blood-libel. (accessed February 2, 2025).

6 Gilbert, L., "A Yom Kippur Blood Libel in New York," *Center for Jewish History*. Available online: https://blog.cjh.org/index.php/2024/10/02/yom-kippur-blood-libel/ (accessed February 2, 2025).

7 "Blood Libel," Holocaust Encyclopedia, *US Holocaust Memorial Museum*. Available online: https://encyclopedia.ushmm.org/content/en/article/blood-libel. (accessed February 2, 2025).

8 "Blood Libel Accusations Resurface in Wake of Oct. 7," International Affairs, *ADL,* January 26, 2024. Available online: https://www.adl.org/resources/article/blood-libel -accusations-resurface-wake-oct-7 (accessed February 2, 2025).

9 Wilf, Einat, "The Palestine Propaganda Complex," *Sapir Journal*, Winter 2024. Available online: https://sapirjournal.org/friends-and-foes/2024/03/the-palestine -propaganda-complex/ (accessed February 2, 2025).

10 Kendi, Ibram. X., *How to be an Antiracist,* One World, New York, 2019.

11 "Ghettos," Holocaust Encyclopedia, *US Holocaust Memorial Museum*. Available online: https://encyclopedia.ushmm.org/content/en/article/ghettos (accessed February 2, 2025).

12 Coren, Michael, "The Reformation at 500: Grappling with Martin Luther's anti-Semitic Legacy," *Maclean's*, October 25, 2017. Available online: https://macleans.ca/ society/the-reformation-at-500-grappling-with-martin-luthers-anti-semitic-legacy/ (accessed February 2, 2025).

13 "The Kidnapping of Edgardo Levi Mortara," *The American Jewish Archive*. Available online: https://www.americanjewisharchives.org/snapshots/the-kidnapping-of -edgardo-levi-mortara/ (accessed February 2, 2025).

14 "A Hoax of Hate: The Protocols of the Learned Elders of Zion," Backgrounder, *ADL,* October 23, 2012. Available online: https://www.adl.org/resources/backgrounder/ hoax-hate-protocols-learned-elders-zion (accessed February 2, 2025).

15 Goldberg, A., "An Interview with Professor Yehuda Bauer," January 18, 1998, 45–46. Available online: https://www.yadvashem.org/odot_pdf/microsoft%20word%20-%20 3856.pdf, 46 (accessed February 2, 2025).

16 Ibid.

17 "Yehuda Bauer (1926–2024)," Biography, *Jewish Virtual Library*. Available online: https://www.jewishvirtuallibrary.org/yehuda-bauer (accessed February 2, 2025).

18 "The ADL Global 100 Index of Antisemitism," *ADL*, January 14, 2025. Available online: https://www.adl.org/adl-global-100-index-antisemitism (accessed February 2, 2025).

19 Exod. 1:8-10.

20 Est. 3:8.

21 Horn, Dara, *People Love Dead Jews*, Horton, New York, 2021, 106–7.

Chapter 3

1 Hernandez, Alma, "The Modern Face of Antisemitism and the Diversity of Jewish Identity," *ABA Human Rights Magazine -2024 December Special Issue: Combating Antisemitism,* December 9, 2024. Available online: https://www.americanbar.org/ groups/crsj/resources/human-rights/2024-december/modern-face-of-antisemitism/ (accessed February 2, 2025).

2 Gen. 32:29.

3 Perry, Mark, "Looking Back at the Remarkable History of the Nobel Prize from 1901–2020 Using Maps, Charts, and Tables," *The American Enterprise Institute*, October 12, 2020. Available online: https://www.aei.org/carpe-diem/looking-back-at -the-remarkable-history-of-the-nobel-prize-from-1901-2020-using-maps-charts-and -tables/ (accessed online February 2, 2025).

4 Exod. 22:21.

5 Exod. 23:9.

6 Lev. 19:18.

7 Lev. 19:33-34.

8 Sacks, Jonathan, "Healing the Heart of Darkness," *Jonathan Sacks: The Rabbi Sacks Legacy*, 2014, 2022. Available online: https://rabbisacks.org/covenant-conversation/ mishpatim/healing-heart-darkness/ (accessed February 2, 2025).

9 Ibid.

Chapter 4

1   Hab. 2:4.

2   Ps. 23:4.

3   Halevi, Judah, *The Kuzari,* c. 1120–1140. Available online: https://www.sefaria.org/Kuzari?tab=contents (accessed February 2, 2025).

4   Shevuoth 30A; Sanhedrin 27B.

5   Halevi, Yehuda, *Selected Poems of Yehuda HaLevi*, trans. Salaman, Nina, 1924, public domain.

Chapter 5

1   Sabbath 31A.

2   Pirkei Avot 2:10.

3   Sifra 89a.

Chapter 6

1   Feigenbaum, Susan, adapted from "Today's Jury Room: A Safe Haven from Bigotry," *The Southern New England Jewish Ledger,* August 30, 2017. Available online: https://www.jewishledger.com/2017/08/kolot-todays-jury-room-safe-haven-bigotry/ (accessed online February 2, 2025).

2   Exod. 13:18.

3   Gen. 14:14.

4   Exod. 14:14.

5   "J7-The Large Communities Task Force Against Antisemitism," *ADL.* Available online: https://www.adl.org/j7-large-communities-task-force-against-antisemitism#:~:text=In%20response%20to%20increasing%20rates,Communities'%20Task%20Force%20Against%20Antisemitism (accessed February 2, 2025).

Chapter 7

1 "Holocaust Survivor Shares Story with Students," *Avon Old Farms School*, November 5, 2019. Available online: https://www.avonoldfarms.com/about/news/news-stories/~board/news/post/holocaust-survivor-shares-story-with-students (accessed February 2, 2025).

2 Risen, Clay, "Yehuda Bauer, 98, Scholar Who Saw Jewish Resistance in Holocaust, Dies," *The New York Times*, October 22, 2024. Available online: https://www.nytimes.com/2024/10/22/world/middleeast/yehuda-bauer-dead.html (accessed February 2, 2025).

3 "Gov. Molloy Signs Law Requiring Holocaust and Genocide Education in Connecticut Schools," *Governor Dannel P. Molloy Archive*, May 10, 2018. Available online: https://portal.ct.gov/malloy-archive/press-room/press-releases/2018/05-2018/gov-malloy-signs-law-requiring-holocaust-and-genocide-education-in-connecticut-schools (accessed February 2, 2025).

4 Connecticut Voices of Hope. Available online: https://www.ctvoicesofhope.org/ (accessed February 2, 2025).

5 US Holocaust Memorial Museum. Available online: https://www.ushmm.org/ (accessed February 2, 2025).

6 Echoes and Reflections. Available online: https://echoesandreflections.org/where-to-begin/?gad_source=1&gclid=CjwKCAiAqfe8BhBwEiwAsne6gf22gp868qecesjsF7johWf0Y9n5OEhfiiwINn90iIQUeOp_oqdR1hoC1zIQAvD_BwE (accessed February 2, 2025).

7 USC Shoah Foundation. Available online: https://sfi.usc.edu/ (accessed February 2, 2025).

8 "Survey Shows Holocaust Education and Survivor Testimony Has Profound Impacts," *USC Shoah Foundation*. Available online: https://sfi.usc.edu/news/2020/09/28761-survey-shows-holocaust-education-and-survivor-testimony-has-profound-impacts (accessed February 2, 2025).

9 "Antisemitic Attitudes in America: Conspiracy Theories, Holocaust Education and Other Predictors of Antisemitic Beliefs," Center for Antisemitism Research, *ADL*, March 17, 2023. Available online: https://www.adl.org/resources/report/antisemitic-attitudes-america-conspiracy-theories-holocaust-education-and-other (accessed February 2, 2025).

10 Ibid.

11 Ibid.

12 Ibid.

13 "The ADL Global 100 Index of Antisemitism," *ADL*, January 14, 2025. Available online: https://www.adl.org/adl-global-100-index-antisemitism (accessed February 2, 2025).

14 "UAE Launches Manara Center to Promote Regional Co-Existence," *ADL*, March 14, 2023. Available online: https://www.adl.org/resources/press-release/uae-launches -manara-center-promote-regional-co-existence?utm_campaign=asbrief2024&utm _medium=email&utm_source=whole&utm_content=e20241121 (accessed February 2, 2025).

Chapter 8

1 Gen. 12:1.

2 Gen. 12:2-3.

3 Gen. 12:7.

4 Gen. 14:13.

5 Gen. 10:24; 11:4.

6 The Rabbinical Assembly, *Etz Hayim: Torah and Commentary*, The Jewish Publication Society, New York, 2001, 79.

7 Cosgrove, Elliott, "Forging a New Vision of American Judaism and American Zionism," *Hadassah Magazine*, September/October 2024. Available online: https:// www.hadassahmagazine.org/2024/09/05/rabbi-elliot-cosgrove-forging-a-new-vision -of-american-judaism-and-american-zionism/ (accessed February 2, 2025).

8 Gen. 22:1-18.

9 2 Chron. 3.

10 Gen. 28:10-15.

11 Gen. 32:23-32.

12 Deut. 31:7.

13 Josh. 1:2-4.

14 Gen. 14:18.

15 Gen. 22:14.

16 2 Sam. 5:7.

17 The Rabbinical Assembly, *Siddur Sim Shalom For Weekdays*, The United Synagogue of Conservative Judaism, New York, 2005, 65-6.

18 Ibid., 66.

19 Ibid., 74.

20 Hostein, Lisa, "Deborah Lipstadt," *Hadassah Magazine*, November/December 2024, 64.

21 "The Covenant of the Islamic Resistance Movement, Hamas Covenant 1988," August 18, 1988. Available online: https://avalon.law.yale.edu/20th_century/hamas.asp (accessed February 2, 2025); Grigat, Stephan, "Antisemitic Anti-Zionism: Muslim Brotherhood, Hezbollah and Iran," *Volume 5, Confronting Antisemitism in Modern Media, the Legal and Political Worlds*, Degruyter, 2021. Available online: https://www .degruyter.com/document/doi/10.1515/9783110671964-010/html?lang=en&srsltid =AfmBOoo7zxIhdRA2xxpxzvi0rRZwJ2BgRxpBjhQiXv6GZPqEk2z-Kylq (accessed February 2, 2025).

Chapter 9

1 Exod. 36:5.

2 Exod. 25:8.

3 Lev. 19:18.

4 Lev. 19:17.

5 Acho, Emmanuel and Tishby, Noa, *Uncomfortable Conversations with a Jew*, Simon & Schuster, New York, 2024, 225.

6 Pirkei Avot 2:4.

7 Ibid.

8 Pirkei Avot 1:14.

9 US National Strategy to Counter Anrtisemitism, 2023, 48. Available online: https:// bidenwhitehouse.archives.gov/wp-content/uploads/2023/05/U.S.-National-Strategy-to -Counter-Antisemitism.pdf (accessed March 11, 2025).

Conclusion and Call to Action

1 Schickman, Mark, "Introduction: Antisemitism: Civil Rights Advocacy is Long Overdue," *ABA Human Rights Magazine—December 2024 Special Issue: Combating*

Antisemitism, December 9, 2024. Available online: https://www.americanbar.org/groups/crsj/resources/human-rights/2024-december/ (accessed February 2, 2024).

2 Biden, Joseph, Preamble Letter, The U.S. National Strategy to Counter Antisemitism, May 2023. Available online: https://bidenwhitehouse.archives.gov/wp-content/uploads/2023/05/U.S.-National-Strategy-to-Counter-Antisemitism.pdf (accessed March 11, 2025).

3 Lipstadt, D. E., *Antisemitism Here and Now*, Schocken Books, New York, 2019, xi.

4 Isa. 58:10.

5 Mal. 2:10.

6 https://www.whitehouse.gov/wp-content/uploads/2023/05/U.S.-National-Strategy-to-Counter-Antisemitism.pdf.

7 "Playing With Hate: How Online Gamers with Diverse Usernames are Treated," Center for Technology and Society, *ADL*, January 16, 2025. Available online: https://www.adl.org/resources/report/playing-hate-how-online-gamers-diverse-identity-usernames-are-treated (accessed February 2, 2025).

8 Gen. 1:3-4.

9 Mic. 6:8.

ABOUT THE AUTHORS

Rabbi Philip Lazowski, Rabbi Emeritus of Beth Hillel Synagogue, Bloomfield, Connecticut, and The Emanuel Synagogue, West Hartford, Connecticut, is affectionately and reverentially known as an educator, writer, and spiritual leader who inspired over three generations. His more than a dozen books have made their way to Jewish and non-Jewish bookshelves and into the broader world. His primary commitment in life is teaching honesty, decency, and justice. As a Holocaust survivor, he creatively and courageously has taught of the horrors inflicted on the Jewish People. He holds degrees from Yeshiva University, New York, USA; Brooklyn College; and the Jewish Theological Seminary, New York, USA. He is Chaplain of the Connecticut State Senate and Hartford Hospital. Additionally, he was the former chaplain of the Hartford Police.

Suzanne Batchelor Pinkes is a retired attorney, Board Chair for the Connecticut Region of the Anti-Defamation League, and a member of ADL's Global Leadership Council.

www.ingramcontent.com/pod-product-compliance
Lightning Source LLC
Chambersburg PA
CBHW060341100426
42812CB00003B/1078